I Am MORE than ENOUGH

I Am **MORE** *than* ENOUGH

HELPING WOMEN SILENCE THEIR INNER CRITIC *and* CELEBRATE THEIR INNER VOICE

Dr. Robert Jones *and* Bryce Dunford

PLAIN SIGHT PUBLISHING
AN IMPRINT OF CEDAR FORT, INC.
SPRINGVILLE, UT

ISBN 13: 978-1-4621-1282-1

Published by Plain Sight Publishing, an imprint of Cedar Fort, Inc
2373 W. 700 S., Springville, UT 84663
Distributed by Cedar Fort, Inc., www.cedarfort.com

LIBRARY OF CONGRESS CATALOGING-IN-PUBLICATION DATA

Jones, Robert, 1950- author.
I am more than enough / Robert Jones, DC, and Bryce Dunford.
   pages cm
Includes bibliographical references and index.
ISBN 978-1-4621-1282-1 (alk. paper)
1. Self-esteem in women. 2. Sex differences (Psychology) I. Dunford, Bryce, 1969- author. II. Title.

BF697.5.S46J66 2013
155.3'3391--dc23

2013033366

Cover design by Angela D. Baxter
Cover design © 2013 by Lyle Mortimer
Edited and typeset by Whitney Lindsley

Printed in the United States of America

10 9 8 7 6 5 4 3 2 1

Printed on acid-free paper

To my wife, Joy, my three daughters—Arian, Ashley, and Kelsey—
and to all my female patients over thirty-two years of practice.
All these women have taught me volumes.

—Robert Jones

To my amazing wife, Jennifer

—Bryce Dunford

contents

acknowledgments

I'd like to acknowledge Bryce Dunford, an amazing teacher and friend. Also James Cox, another incredible teacher and close friend who has taught me more than any other person about life and living.

—*Robert Jones*

There are so many people who have contributed to this book. Too many to list here. I would like to thank a few who have done more than others, in particular, my amazing wife, Jennifer. Her kindness, patience, and insight has been the biggest influence of them all. Thanks also to the following, without whose support this project could not have happened: Blaine and Michelle Anderson, Jared Halls, John and Tawni Carper, Earl and Annette Jolley, Bruce and Cindy Groesbeck, Linda and Rob Oar, Jeff Johnson, and Spencer Thaxton. More than anything else, I hope this book will be a blessing to the countless women in my life who are far more than enough. They just need to believe it.

—*Bryce Dunford*

introduction

Very suspicious. A book *for* and *about* women written by two *men*. Very suspicious indeed. Or maybe audacious?

We don't think so. Many women might say, "Who do they think they are, writing a book about women? They don't know anything about what we go through. How dare they!"

On the other hand, a similar book written by a woman could bring comments like, "Who does she think she is, anyway? Like she doesn't have any of these issues at all! She's just like *all* the rest of us."

A catch-22. So we wrote.

Being men, we thought that we might be slightly more objective on one of the most difficult of all women's issues. We are more removed from the situation, so it might be a tiny bit easier for us to see what's going on.

One of us has spent over thirty years in practice sitting across a desk from thousands of women discussing their hormone and health problems, from PMS to menopause, and from chronic fatigue to obesity and depression. The other has been teaching adolescents and college-age women for twenty years, seeing their issues and hearing their comments about themselves. Between us we have two wonderful wives and seven wonderful daughters. It is for them, and women like them, that we have written this book. So that they will believe, once and for all, that they really are enough.

Enough is an interesting word. If you look it up in the dictionary, you will come across curious definitions:

- Sufficient
- Adequate
- Passable
- Satisfactory

Frankly, we are all *more* than that—*more* than enough. We are more than adequate. It's just that sometimes, or most of the time, we have such a hard time admitting it to ourselves (let alone to others).

We would certainly like to believe that we are more than enough. But that voice inside us—that has probably been there since we were small—stops us from thinking much good about ourselves.

The greatest secret on earth is to control our own minds and the voices within them. To this end is this book written.

> Our deepest fear is not that we are inadequate. Our deepest fear is that we are powerful beyond measure. It is our light, not our darkness that most frightens us. We ask ourselves, Who am I to be brilliant, gorgeous, talented, fabulous? Actually, who are you not to be? You are a child of God. Your playing small does not serve the world. There is nothing enlightened about shrinking so that other people won't feel insecure around you. We are all meant to shine, as children do. We were born to make manifest the glory of God that is within us. It's not just in some of us; it's in everyone. And as we let our own light shine, we unconsciously give other people permission to do the same. As we are liberated from our own fear, our presence automatically liberates others.[1]

The road to self-discovery is painful, but it is not as painful as not knowing for the rest of your life how great you really were. You *are* more than enough.

As authors, we worried a little in the beginning about how the topic of this book would be received by women. So we held focus groups. We interviewed women and got feedback from them and from other female authors regarding whether there was a need for this book. The response was overwhelmingly positive. Many women wanted the book not only for themselves, but also for their daughters—because they didn't want their daughters going through the same things they had gone through.

We asked questions—so many questions—to women and the men who love them. Questions like these:

- Do you like yourself?
- Why do you have so many self-deprecating thoughts during the day?
- Do you believe every thing you tell yourself about yourself?
- What is the payoff for being so mean to yourself?
- From where do you derive your worth?
- How many times a day do you compare yourself with others, and why do you do it?
- How do you feel when you find yourself in a martyr role?
- What triggers you to go into your "dark place"?
- Why do you consider yourself to be a perfectionist?
- Do you have a hard time being honest with yourself *and* others?
- Why do you have a hard time facing the truth about yourself?
- When you are in a group of women, what thoughts are going through your head? Have you analyzed why?
- Are you a mind reader of others?
- How does your thinking change when you are tired?
- Have you ever thought that you have hormonal imbalances?
- How does procrastinating help you?
- Who would you be and how would you feel without all these self-demeaning, sometimes self-destructive thoughts?

These and many other questions are the ones we have been asking women for years. Don't get us wrong; we men have our own issues, which we will address in an abbreviated version as it applies to women, but our scope is to deal with women's issues as it affects their *minds*. That is where this battle must be fought and won.

This book is not "fluff." It's not meant to be a feel good, rah-rah, "you-can-do-it" book that you can just browse through and then put on the shelf. Some of the things we write about in this book may be painful. This book is meant to change your thinking about yourself by actually *doing* things. It will be hard-hitting at times as we challenge your thoughts about yourself. Once you read this book and actually let it affect you, you will never think the same or be the same again.

Come join us on this intimate journey of changing your thoughts so you can change your life. We dare you!

NOTE

1.   Marianne Williamson, *A Return To Love: Reflections on the Principles of A Course in Miracles*, (Harper Collins, 1992), 190.

Part One

one

MEN'S WEAKNESS/ WOMEN'S WEAKNESS

Human beings are incredible!
Our history is filled with inspiring stories of love, courage, sacrifice, forgiveness, dedication, and other great qualities. Not enough paper exists in the world to chronicle the goodness of mankind. But this is not the story of our strengths. This is the story of our weakness. Not our individual shortcomings, but the weakness of our genders. Men are broken in a very common way, as are women. Each gender has an Achilles heel, a natural weakness that seems to be programmed into our very DNA.

If you'd like to see both weaknesses for yourself, find a crowded room where both men and women are entering, without knowing others in the room—a public meeting, a classroom on the first day of school, the DMV. After a man sits down, he will begin to check out the room. If you watch his eyes, you will notice that he is looking at all the beautiful women. His eyes will usually settle on one woman, the one he thinks is the most beautiful—and he will glance at her again and again. That is how men are programmed. He's looking for the most beautiful woman in the room, and the more he looks at her, the more excited he is to be in the same room.

Women are programmed differently. A woman will take her seat and will also check out the room. You might suspect that she is looking at the men, perhaps searching for the best-looking man in the room. She is not. If you watch her eyes, you will discover that she is *also* looking at the women around her, but for a very different reason.

She is noticing all those who are prettier than she is: younger, thinner, more organized, better dressed. Aware of and sensitive to what she perceives as her weaknesses, she naturally notices those who have strengths in areas where she sees only deficiencies in herself. A woman who thinks she is overweight will instantly notice all the skinny women in the room. A woman who questions her abilities as a mother will notice the women whose children seem so well behaved or so well dressed. The more she glances at these other women, the more discouraged she feels to be in the same room.

Here's the conversation in her head:

"Look at her hair. That's *exactly* the way I wish mine would go. I'll bet she's a size 4—no—maybe a 2. And look at that dress! I wonder where she found that. I *knew* I should have worn my red outfit. Look at her skin; it's flawless. I'm going to try a new makeup line. I shouldn't even be here. I don't belong with people like this. . . ." That is how women are programmed. Though they do so many things well, and have countless admirable qualities, women have a natural tendency to think less of themselves, to see their flaws and weaknesses, to tear themselves down, to ruthlessly compare themselves to others. Women are naturally inclined to think they are not good enough.

Ponder for a moment your five greatest strengths or best qualities. If we asked you to write them down, how long would you take to compile the list? Now think of your greatest weaknesses or flaws. How much more quickly does that list come to your mind? Which list is longer? Which list is on your mind most frequently? If you kept score and counted your thoughts about yourself, how many of them are positive and focused on your strengths, and how many are negative and focused on your flaws?

You're not alone. Just about every other woman on this planet is doing the exact same thing. Negative thoughts about herself are as common in a woman as sexual thoughts are in a man.

We have interviewed enough women to say confidently that when you find that you are comparing yourself to another woman, that woman is comparing herself to someone also—perhaps even you. Maybe you notice the woman who is always dressed so well with such distinguished clothes. She makes you think that your wardrobe is so boring and plain and that your clothes don't fit very well.

You start getting down on yourself. What you don't realize is that that woman is noticing what an amazing mother you are and is getting down on herself for not doing the things you do. Or she's noticing some other amazing quality that you possess.

You probably read that last sentence and thought to yourself, "But I don't have any amazing qualities. Why would anyone notice me?" See, that's exactly what we're talking about.

The good news is that you can change your thoughts. You can free yourself of this natural tendency to think less of yourself. You can eliminate the negative thoughts and emotions that affect your day-to-day happiness and the happiness of those around you. You are enough. You are *more* than enough.

THE WEAKNESS

We refer to these two natural tendencies— the tendency of men to sexual arousal and the tendency of women to self-doubt— as *weaknesses*, or Men's Weakness and Women's Weakness. A weakness is an impairment of health or a condition of abnormal functioning. Before you argue that both of these are very "normal"—meaning that they are extremely common—let us make a case for how abnormal they are, and exactly what an impairment of health they can each be.

First, we'll start with Men's Weakness. Is it abnormal? Does it impair health?

Let's compare a man's appetite for sex with his appetite for food. The biological purpose of eating is to refuel our bodies and the biological purpose of sex is to procreate. If a man ate whenever he desired and as much as he desired, he'd certainly overeat. But not by much.

He would never, in one sitting, eat ten times what his body required. In other words, his appetite is in relative proportion to its purpose; it is normal. It's what we call self-limiting.

However, if a man gave into his sexual urges every time he felt the desire and if each of these encounters resulted in a baby, in the span of ten years he might easily populate a small town. In the words of C. S. Lewis, "This appetite is in ludicrous and preposterous excess of its function"; it is very abnormal.[1]

Hence, we call it Men's *Weakness*.

Does it impair health? We call to the witness stand the countless women and children who have been betrayed, cheated on, abused, demeaned, taken advantage of, and hurt at the hands of the male sex drive. How many hearts have been broken or pierced with deep wounds by an uncontrolled husband, father, brother, son, friend, or partner?

The fact that a man's inclination for sex is "natural" does not make it any less damaging when left uncontrolled.

Likewise, the fact that women seem naturally inclined to compare themselves to others does not make the negative self-talk that results from the comparison any less damaging to their mental and emotional health.

What makes Women's Weakness "abnormal" is the curious fact that the way a woman treats herself is so uncharacteristic of how she treats almost every other person in her life. By nature, women are often kind, caring, compassionate, and forgiving. The very act of giving birth is a marvelous symbol of the nature of most women. They risk their life, their health, and their comfort for their child.

Yet those same women can be so cruel toward themselves and so unmercifully demanding. It's abnormal. It's a weakness. It's Women's Weakness.

I [Bryce] have an unexplainable habit of forgetting to start the dishwasher after I've loaded it full of dirty dishes. I put the soap in, shut the dispenser, close the dishwasher, but then I forget to start it. I don't do it on purpose, and even being aware of my tendency, I still do it.

My wife's reaction? She laughs. It has certainly inconvenienced her on more than one occasion, yet she thinks it's hilarious that an ordinarily intelligent man could be so consistently forgetful. In other words, she is kind and patient with my flaws, even when my forgetfulness puts her out. But she is not as forgiving nor as kind with her own imperfections. Rather than laughing at them, her shortcomings often drag her down into a pit of discouragement.

Does Women's Weakness impair health? Perhaps one of the many accounts we have gathered will serve to demonstrate. We asked a group of women to write their own obituary, one woman penned the following:

> In thinking about this assignment, I realized that I had a wonderful obituary—up until about three years ago. Until then, I was at the top of my profession, with a prestigious title; I was actively involved in the community, with a prestigious title; I had been married for 31 years, another prestigious title (wife); and I had three wonderful, well adjusted children; the best prestigious title (Mom).
>
> Now, the economy has killed my professional life so that I am virtually unemployed. I no longer have time for community involvement, and my marriage ended.
>
> I still have the title of Mom, but my ex-husband has remarried a wonderful woman who could easily step into my shoes.
>
> "I have to wonder if the mom I have become is actually hurtful to my kids. They knew me as happy, successful, grounded. What they see now is creating new memories of me that I would prefer they not have.
>
> I feel that I am wasted space. I am taking up oxygen for no good reason. If my obituary ended three years ago, I would have left a wonderful legacy of memories and examples for my children. Now, the page is blank.
>
> My passing is remarked by no sign, no evidence. Not even a footprint.

ELECTRICAL AND CHEMICAL

Women's Weakness can be broken into two parts: one lasts for just a brief moment, and the other can last for a painfully long time.

In fact, both Men's Weakness and Women's Weakness have these same two components and understanding these elements is critical to overcoming our natural tendencies. The first part is electrical, and the second part is chemical.

Thoughts are electrical. They come and go at the speed of electricity. They are easily changed but must be changed quickly before they escalate into something else. The moment a thought pops into your head is a critical moment. You have just a brief instant to decide what you are going to do with that thought. That instant holds the key to your freedom from these natural weaknesses.

If thoughts are allowed to linger, they begin to trigger all sorts of hormones—chemicals—that are released into your bloodstream. These hormones stir deep emotions. The electrical problem (what you were thinking) has now become a chemical problem (what you are now feeling) and chemicals don't go away quickly or easily, nor do the emotions they trigger. It is still possible to win the battle, but it is more difficult at this stage.

Have you ever been in a conversation with someone when they said something that was either upsetting or embarrassing to you? What did you feel? A flushing feeling coursing through your body? Maybe your heart started beating more quickly, or you turned red. Maybe you just wanted to run away. Those are all chemical reactions in your body, caused by different hormones from the adrenal glands.

I could just feel myself . . .

- Getting angry
- Turning red
- Feeling upset
- Wanting to cry
- Wanting to beat myself up
- Getting rattled
- Wanting to lash out
- Wanting to hide

These are all emotions caused by the change of the electric thought into a chemical. Of course, those released chemicals in the bloodstream can keep us out of harm's way (like walking down a dark alley while hearing footsteps behind us makes our hearts beat and makes us able to run, really fast), but more often than not, those chemicals lead us into some very unwanted and nasty emotions.

Let's use Men's Weakness to illustrate how this process usually works:

A man is walking down the street and sees a beautiful woman with a low-cut top. BAM! A thought enters his head. It's a sexual thought. They come so naturally and so frequently into the men's minds. At this moment the man has a critical choice: he can either take control of the thought and remove it or change it, or he can let it linger and escalate. The electrical portion of Men's Weakness is much easier to control, but the time frame in which he takes action is much shorter. Thoughts have to be controlled instantaneously or else they will quickly become emotions.

Let's suppose that he lets the thought linger. It becomes another thought, more sexual in nature, and quickly another. Pretty soon, his body starts to release hormones into his bloodstream. Now he's aroused. The electrical thoughts have turned into chemical emotions. Now he has a whole new battle on his hands. Emotions can be changed, but they are much more difficult to change than thoughts. If they are not changed, they can lead to serious problems. Men make dumb decisions while they are sexually aroused. If this man is not careful and he lets his emotions continue to escalate, his Men's Weakness is going to hurt him and the people he loves.

Women's Weakness functions the same way. It all starts with a thought. You look at yourself in a mirror and a thought pops into your head. You pick up a magazine with airbrushed photos of ultra-thin models, and a thought pops into your head. You see a picture of yourself, you volunteer at your child's school with other mothers, you go to the grocery store, you attend a meeting at work, and thoughts pop into your head. They come so easily and naturally. They are the ones that say, "You are not good enough." They make you think that all the other women in the world are so much more beautiful, so much more successful than you.

Now you are in the same position as the man with the sexual thought. This is a critical moment, but it will only last for a brief instant. You can take control of that thought—throw it out, change it, remove it—or you can let it linger and escalate.

If those self-demeaning thoughts are allowed to linger in your mind, they begin to trigger all sorts of hormones, which in turn stir up emotions. Sometimes this emotional reaction is mild—you get upset, frustrated, embarrassed, down on yourself. Other times these emotions continue to escalate into a deep, dark, ugly abyss.

One woman described these dark emotions as follows:

> It's like being in the ocean on the edge of a giant whirlpool that is swirling around and down into a funnel. Suddenly I get sucked in and begin to swirl around the funnel. Around and around and around. Each time I go around, I get sucked in deeper and deeper. It gets darker and darker. I feel like I'm drowning, I can't breathe. If I go all the way, I find myself at the bottom of this dark funnel, feeling completely helpless to get out.

We have spoken to hundreds of women about this funnel. Several call it "the dark side." One described it as being in a dark cave with no light; another as though her heart was being wound with cords, suffocating her emotionally. However, every woman with whom we have spoken knows that dark side. It appears to be a common element of Women's Weakness. Husbands and children all seem to know when mom is in the funnel. Some women have confessed to spending a great deal of time in the funnel, others only occasionally. Like their male counterparts, many women have admitted that they have made some pretty dumb decisions during these dark emotional episodes. Things were said that were harsh and painful to others and were later deeply regretted. One woman declared that she almost married a man that was not right for her because at the time she thought so little of herself and did not believe that she deserved anyone better.

Part two of this book will provide several suggestions on how to "keep it electrical," or how to prevent electrical thoughts from becoming chemical emotions (see chapter 8). Studies have been done with pornography addicts that show that they can be successful in overcoming a powerful mind addiction by training themselves to immediately start asking certain questions as they have the urges to view pornography. This also works for women who are likewise addicted to improper thinking about themselves.

We assert that both Men's Weakness and Women's Weakness are curable, or perhaps more accurately stated, controllable. Maybe we'll never rid them from our system, but they need not control our lives, nor tarnish our happiness.

APPLES TO ORANGES: THE EPIDEMIC OF COMPARISON SICKNESS

The lies we tell ourselves can be crippling. Women's minds seem to be preprogrammed for comparison. We call it *Comparison Sickness.* The constant tendency to compare oneself to others is unhealthy and unfair. Nevertheless, it happens constantly in a woman's mind all day long. Yes, men compare themselves too, but come to a different conclusion: "I'm good. I'm okay. I'm better." We'll see in another chapter how this begins physiologically from the moment a little girl is born. That's why we say this "weakness" is epidemic in proportion.

Comparing is, no doubt, natural—a human trait. But when we do so, we often compare our weakest qualities with someone else's strengths. That is not fair and the consequences of comparing oneself to others with a constant downward result or outcome are not good for anyone.

In an address titled "Notwithstanding My Weakness," author/speaker Neal Maxwell talked at length about how we judge ourselves:

> Some of us who would not chastise a neighbor for his frailties have a field day with our own. Some of us stand before no more harsh a judge than ourselves, a judge who stubbornly refuses to admit much happy evidence and who cares nothing for due process. . . . We can allow for the reality that God is more concerned with growth than with geography.[2]

COMPARISON SICKNESS

Have you ever compared yourself with someone like Mother Teresa? Marie Curie? Miss America? How did you come out on that one? That's exactly where "an apples to oranges comparison" arises. These comparisons have no even standards and involve comparing two things that are so different that they can't even be compared fairly or accurately. And yet we do it all the time.

Let's define *comparison sickness* so you can tell us if you might have some of the signs and symptoms. This sickness is diagnosed by the following: whenever you see another person you *automatically* begin comparing yourself to him or her—usually your worst to his or her best. Sound familiar? If it does, you have the weakness at least part of the time. Some women have it full-time, and, as we have seen and heard in past focus groups we have led, it is driving these women crazy.

Wise indeed is the following statement,

"Why compare yourself with others? No one in the entire world can do a better job of being you—than you." (Unknown)

We all tend to compare ourselves to others and try to estimate where we stand based on what we see them doing. If it were merely a simple observation of another person and it ended there, that would be fine. But often we can't leave it there, and it becomes a pathological judgment of ourselves. As stated above, there is no harsher person to judge us than ourselves.

It doesn't matter how many "cheerleaders" you have rooting for you. If you're not on your own side, you usually tend to lose the game. And that is the problem with comparing: it's almost always a losing game for women and you end up, in your mind, just not measuring up.

Maybe it comes from our minds' incessant need to quantify things. We find that we need to categorize or classify ourselves so we know exactly where we belong in life. We have to know where we fit in. If we don't know where we fit in, or how we "stack up" against others, we feel uncomfortable in some way. It is this constant quantification that gets us into trouble in our heads.

Imagine attending your twenty-fifth high school reunion. These reunions have always been the classic setup for comparisons. When we ask women, "Why do you want to go to your high school reunion?" they generally say they want to "see their old friends." When we probe more deeply, they admit that they are going because they want to see how everyone else is doing in life: "So you want to see how they are doing—basically so you can compare yourself to them to see if you have succeeded and hoping maybe that they are not as successful in life as you are? Is that it?"

"Oh, no—I just want to see my old friends."

"And when you see your old friends what do you talk about?"

"Uh, well, we talk about our husbands, our jobs, how many children we have, what they're doing in life—things like that."

"And *why* do you ask them those things?"

"Yeah, I see where you're going with this. I guess it really is all about how I stack up against my old friends. I guess I just want to know if I'm okay."

Ah, yes. The "okay" factor. In whose mind should you be okay? Theirs or yours? Yours is really the only one that really matters. Would it surprise you to know that your old friends at the reunion are going through the same comparison routine you are and they are hoping against hope that they are "okay" too? It shouldn't.

Now don't think that we are against going to reunions. By their very nature, however, they are designed to set us up to compare ourselves to others. Reunions are a glaring example of being in a situation where we are constantly comparing. But in actuality, don't we go through many "mini-reunions" many times per week? Think of going to work, church, the PTA meeting, the gym, or the grocery store. We meet people we haven't seen for a while and our minds quickly go into comparison mode. It might even be with someone that we just saw yesterday. It's what we do afterward that really hurts us or helps us internally.

If we are aware of our thoughts *before* we enter into each of these mini-reunions each day, we can master our thinking and our emotions. We will see the situation for what it is—not a time to measure ourselves and see how we stack up against another—but rather a time to enjoy who we are, "warts and all." The key is to be mindful. Let's examine this word, *mindful*. It is an extremely important word. Mindfulness is to be aware of what you are thinking. Put another way, it is "thinking about what you are thinking about." Mindfulness is a state of active, open attention on the present. When you're mindful, you observe your thoughts and feelings from a distance. Instead of letting your life pass you by, mindfulness means living in the moment and awakening to experience.

In the second half of this book we will suggest tools that can help you to overcome the need to compare yourselves to others; help you rid yourselves of these unhealthy, unproductive, unwanted thought-habits; and help you be mindful. This type of constant comparison leaves one mentally fatigued. When that mental fatigue sets in, you cannot, in your mind, ever be "enough."

The following example is one we have used in many focus groups and speeches to women's groups. It is always amazing for us to see women's reactions to this story. They almost always ask, "How did you get inside my head?"

Muriel walked into the PTA meeting promptly at seven o'clock. There were several empty seats on the front row, so she took one. She had a fourth grader and a sixth grader attending the school, and she felt she needed to keep up on all the happenings of the school scene. It had been a great day for her and she was in a cheerful mood as she glanced around the room. She was excited to be there and wanted to be more involved as a mother.

(Now let's watch what happens inside Muriel's head as the meeting proceeds.)

A woman stood up and began the meeting. *Wow*, Muriel thought to herself. *That's a beautiful outfit. I think I'm really underdressed for the occasion.*

The first speaker talked about the new program to increase test scores in the students. "The average score on the sixth grade level was 86 percent. We're all so excited about how well our students placed!"

Muriel then remembered that her son, Michael, had scored a 64 percent. Ugh!

(Now watch her first thought.)

"I'm really failing as a mother. I should be spending more time with Michael after school. 86 percent? He has so far to go. If only I would have started with him back in second grade."

The next speaker talked about the need for more volunteers in the classrooms to help with the new reading program. Muriel felt like the speaker was looking right at her. She noticed Michael's teacher to her right a few rows back. Now the guilt set in.

I don't know why I even came to this meeting tonight, she thought. *I neglect my kids. I can't even get a meal cooked for my husband. I wonder if anyone would notice if I got up and left right now. Why did I sit on the front row?*

By this time, she was frowning and hardly paying attention to the speaker.

(Now let's jump into the mind of the speaker, Mary)

Mary was talking about the new reading program that she headed up for the PTA. As she was speaking, she glanced down at Muriel and saw the look on her face. Several of the other women were talking on the back row, not paying much attention to her.

A lot of good I'm doing here, she thought to herself. *Nobody is listening. This lady on the front row looks irritated. Under my leadership the new reading program is failing. What am I doing here? I think I'll just leave after I do my part. Besides, the teachers should really be the ones to do this. I think I'm going to resign.*

(Now let's look into the mind of the PTA president, sitting on the front row also.)

She thought to herself, *"Mary sure has her stuff together. We just handed her the reading program and she ran with it. Sure wish we had more like her. Look at her hair. I wonder who does it. I can't stand my style—it's so outdated. Mary must be a size 2. I'd give anything to fit into an outfit like that. It seems like Mary has so many friends. I don't think I have even one really good friend. Why am I doing this? Let's see, I have three more months to serve—then I'm outta here. Can't wait. I'm so ineffective . . ."*

And on it goes. Look at the things they are telling themselves—many lies.

The fact is, Muriel is a *wonderful* mother; her children love her and she loves them. Her home life is wonderful. A 64 percent does not make a bad mother. Michael is so successful in every other facet of his life.

Everybody envies Mary—except Mary. She sees herself in a totally different light. Nobody else *dared* take on the new reading program. It's actually going much better than the principal had ever imagined, all due to Mary's leadership. But Mary doesn't see the good she has accomplished.

In her mind, the PTA president is not doing a good job and can't wait to get out. Most of the women admire the PTA president and think she does a wonderful job. The PTA has never been so organized as it has been this year. But she *is* a size 12.

NOTES

1.   C. S. Lewis, *Mere Christianity*, (New York: HarperCollins, 1952), 89.

2.   Neal A. Maxwell, "Notwithstanding My Weakness, *Ensign*, Nov. 1976, 13.

two

FEMALE BIOLOGY
AND THE BRAIN

Let's take a quick look at some possible reason for women thinking the way they do and why (1) it's so much different than the way men think, and (2) why their biology can have a tremendous impact on why they might be so inherently hard on themselves. In other words, could their DNA in any way affect their self-image or self-esteem?

It's a common occurrence at my clinic to have women come in to consult me [Robert] about the fact that they turn into a completely different person for the five to seven days before their menstrual period begins. They hate themselves, don't want to even be around the persons they love the most, and see only a dark future. Not surprisingly, as soon as they begin their period, almost immediately, the future is brighter and the people around them magically change. Hormones.

What effect could this have on a woman over and over again every month from when she is thirteen to when she is fifty-one (the average age of the onset of menopause)? Do hormonal fluctuations affect her brain? Absolutely. They can actually affect her reality, her moods, and her beliefs about herself and others.

Each phase in a woman's life has a different balance of hormones:

infant, childhood, adolescence, young adult, motherhood, perimeno-pause, menopause, and postmenopause. Nothing constant like a man's changes, which would be like watching concrete wear down as cars drive over it—imperceptible at best.

Structurally there is only about a 1 percent difference between the male and female brains. But that 1 percent is huge. Over the past twenty years we have learned much from MRIs and PET scans of brains in men and women.

These studies and others can help you as a woman understand more of why you do things the way you do. This is crucial to under-standing, for instance, why you may be so sensitive to others' com-ments or someone's tone of voice.

FACT: On average, even after accounting for body sizes, a man's brain is about 9 percent larger than a woman's brain, *but* women have the same number of brain cells as a man. (Some might conclude this means a man's brain is filled with more air, which we think most men will readily admit.)

FACT: Women suffer from depression more than men in a ratio of 2:1. This does not seem to be cultural; it's worldwide. Childhood depression seems to be at a 1:1 ratio. Women pull ahead at the onset of puberty. Hormones? In the menstruating woman there can be up to a 25 percent change in the brain every month.[1]

For instance, MRIs show that the hippocampus (the part of the brain that accounts for memory and emotions) is larger in a woman's brain.[2] Likewise, the area of the brain that controls language and seeing emotions in others is more developed in the female brain. Not surprisingly, a man's brain has almost two and a half times more space for sex drive, action, and aggression. No wonder a man may be think-ing about sex when his wife "just wants to talk." Our brains are hard-wired differently.[3]

Putting this into perspective, researcher Louann Brizendine, MD, a neuropsychiatrist at the University of California, San Fran-cisco, writes, "Sexual thoughts float through a man's brain every fifty-two seconds on average, and through a woman's only once a day."[4]

Question: Is the sex of a fetus male or female from the moment of conception? Up until the fetus is eight to nine weeks old, the forming little thing we call a brain is the brain of a little girl. At about nine weeks that little brain, because of the Y chromosome (genetic coding) will flip a switch and the body starts secreting a hormone called testosterone. If there is no secretion of testosterone, you have a little baby girl seven months later. If the testosterone keeps coming, it's a boy. Then all the differences between boys and girls, men and women, begin to surface.

Now comes the fascinating part that may explain many things to you as a woman regarding why you do some of the things you do. We'll give you a few examples of differences between little girls and little boys that can make *huge* differences in the grown-up versions.

Many years ago childhood researchers thought that all babies had the ability to stare back at a mother's face—a behavior called "facial gazing." As it turns out, baby girls are programmed to do it—baby boys not so much. In the uterus, the female fetus is bathed with estrogens; boys get the testosterone. The estrogens bathe the communication and emotional centers in the brain. The testosterone diminishes those centers in the male fetus. This means that in the first ninety days of the baby girls' life, she can facial gaze nearly 400 percent more than a little boy.[5]

As the little girl grows, she starts picking up on every nuance of her mother's face, and others' as well. She can see the slightly upturned lips of a smile or the slightly furrowed brow. Pretty soon she knows that if she does a certain behavior, Mommy smiles. If she displays another behavior, Mommy frowns. If she sees a blank face, she will try to get a reaction from that face. Think of how these things impact a woman throughout her life ("If I please him, maybe he'll like me more").

But it doesn't stop there. Further studies from Brizendine show that the estrogen bath the fetus gets, and the subsequent amount of estrogen secreted, wires her brain somehow for being able to distinguish auditory tones better than a baby boy.[6] Even at a young age, she can pick up on changes of inflection in her mother's voice. The baby boy can't hear those subtle differences like the female baby. This might explain why, when they were younger, our sons wouldn't listen as well when we say, "Brandon, don't you touch that!" The tones seemed to always stop the daughters but didn't faze the sons. Could this be why, as an adult, a woman is much more tuned in to how another woman talks to her about her hair? Or her outfit? ("I wonder what she meant by *that* comment?")

So right out of the chute (the birth canal), females can read faces better than men; they can hear differences in speech better than men. They are more interested in the cross section of those two: it's called *intimate communication*. She is constantly analyzing content from her earliest years. She compares what she is seeing with what she is hearing. She gathers meaning from faces, words, and actions. Men? They may be thinking about the carburetor. They don't see the same things nor hear the same way as the female. Estrogen versus testosterone—different from the very beginning. Here's a perfect example:

> One of my patients gave her three-and-a-half-year-old daughter many unisex toys, including a bright red fire truck instead of a doll. She walked into her daughter's room one afternoon to find her cuddling the truck in a baby blanket, rocking it back and forth saying, "Don't worry, little truckie, everything will be all right."[7]

Because of the estrogen bath, a Harvard study showed that baby girls become more familiar with their mothers than baby boys do and respond better when the mother tries to calm them down.[8]

Brizendine even postulates, "Disorders that inhibit people from picking up on social nuance—called autism spectrum disorders and Asperger's syndrome—are eight times more common in boys."[9]

Could this be why women, in general, tend to be more empathic, nurturing, and understanding, than their testosterone-laden boyfriends and husbands? Maybe so.

But how does this affect how a woman thinks about herself later on in life? Would this knowledge give a woman time to pause and realize that there is a huge hormonal component to why she does what she does *to herself* from birth? Again, it's hardwired in.

She compares herself to others. She notices every little voice inflection in her phone conversation with her best friend. She analyzes. She's trying to fit it because that's what her hormones taught her to do for self-preservation; for community. She might be passive instead of properly assertive, because that is the hardwiring; it's the default setting of the brain. But when that hardwiring leads a woman to self-deprecating, self-loathing, self-hating thoughts, it becomes counterproductive, no matter what the hardwiring tells her to do.

The point of all this "baby talk" is that genetically a woman may be predisposed to certain behaviors, just like men are. But genetics loads the gun. Someone has to pull the trigger, and we have far too many women pulling the triggers of low self-worth, low self-esteem, and low self-image. Call it whatever you want. It is epidemic, but it can be controlled—permanently.

THE EARLY YEARS

Whether we call it low self-esteem, low self-image, or low self-worth, they all have the same thing in common: "low self." Yes, we suppose there are subtle differences in those three words, but rather than play psychological semantics, for our purposes in this book we feel they are pretty much the same—they imply a faulty way of looking at ourselves that ends up doing damage to ourselves. As we have seen above, it can begin with hormones in utero, but all the research we see in current and past literature point to the fact that by the time a child is six to eight years old, his or her view of self is set.

Somehow we get the idea or belief that we are unlovable, unworthy, substandard, defective, or flawed. Unfortunately, this seems to be rampant throughout the world. Why is it so common?

Notice we said that these are beliefs. We can *believe* that the sun won't come up tomorrow morning. Just because we believe it doesn't make it true. We can therefore believe in things that are false, especially if those things are infused into our brains at a tender age.

So from where do those false beliefs come? They are almost always from the people who raise us—the ones with which we have the most frequent interactions between birth and eight years old, hence the importance of the family—and especially the parents. Yet most parents truly love their kids and would do anything in their power to help them succeed in life.

So what happens?

Most parents are not even mindful of the fact that their four-year-old son or daughter is establishing a self-image founded on the exchanges and dealings they have with mother or father. Certainly the parents' motives are pure, but again, they are not cognizant of the fact that the words they might be using are imperceptibly, invisibly, creating a picture in that child's head about his or her value, lovability, or ranking in the world about them. Even when the parents *are* sensitive to this, they can still have a difficult time stopping their own behavior. They're dealing with "their own issues" so they don't have the skills to help their children form good images of themselves.

An example might be when little Timmy comes home with a poor grade on a math test, his mother comments, "Why can't you be more like your big sister? She gets A's on all her math tests." Timmy may appear to shrug it off, but it may have left an indelible mark on his heart.

Or how about the father that tells his daughter that she'd better study hard in school and get by with her brain in life rather than by her looks. That may sound harsh, but it happens. The father's intent may have been to motivate his daughter, but it could instead devastate her self-image.

I know a woman who bought her daughter a subscription to a teen magazine for her twelfth birthday. Just as she's heading into puberty, that girl will be bombarded by articles and images that make her reevaluate her worth by worldly standards.

And so the problems perpetuate themselves. The parent with low self-esteem passes it on to his or her child. This may explain the age-old biblical passage, "the sins of the parents will be upon the heads of the children."

As a child, you may have been told something by a hurried parent that gave you the impression that you were not quite good enough, not lovable enough. "Could this really be true about me?"

Based on either a misinterpretation of *what* your parent said, or based on an unkind action from some other caregiver, you may begin to believe it. Then you searched the data banks of your child brain to find evidence or proof that what they said about you was true. The data banks have numerous other occasions that validate that you are defective or unlovable.

Add together many of these episodes over the years between birth and eight years old, and what was once only a *belief* (remember, *you can believe things that are not true*) now becomes reality. By the time you are eight, you acquiesce to the beliefs and you accept them as fact about yourself.

Imagine a five-year-old little boy thinking to himself, "If Mommy and Daddy don't like me, there must be a good reason for it." One time won't a poor self-image make, but repeated occurrences over time will certainly make an impact. These feelings about oneself will then remain with a person to the grave unless something is done about it now.

Low self-worth or low self-esteem is not just found in those who are apparent "losers" in life. Many of the rich and famous, either in the business world or in Hollywood (the so-called "successful" people in life), suffer from poor self-image. Few of these people admit to being phony, being pretenders; rather, they are constantly worried about "being discovered." On the outside, they are successful. On the inside, they feel they don't deserve success; it's only a matter of time before everyone knows the truth. These people don't enjoy life any more than any other person with low self-esteem.

By now it should be obvious why so many people have low self-esteem. Brain biology starts it—hormonal fluctuations could make it worse. Throw into the mix our parents' child-rearing fiascoes (even those well intentioned). Conversations around the dinner table each evening could make or break a child's self-esteem. One television program could give a child a distorted sense of self. A teacher at school could make a comment to a child that could steer them into a wonderful career, or could cause them to think they will never be successful. Every event in our lives shapes the way that we think about ourselves and molds us into what we are.

But we can change this. It is *never* too late. As you will read in the second half of this book, there are answers. There is hope. We can indeed alter our course, and that process can begin today.

NOTES

1.　C. S. Woolley, "Sex steroids and Neuronal Growth in Adulthood," *Hormones, Brain and Behavior*, no. 4 (2002): 717–78.

2. C. S. Wolley et al., "Estradiol Increases the Frequency of Multiple Synapse Boutons in the Hippocampal Ca 1 Region of the Adult Female Rat," *Journal of Comparative Neurology* (1996): 108–17.

3.　E.R. Gizewski et al. "Gender-Specific Cerebral Activation during Cognitive Tasks Using Functional MRI: Comparison of Women in Mid-Luteal Phase And Men," *Neuroradiology*, (2006): 14–20.

4.　Louann Brizendine, *The Female Brain* (New York: Morgan Road Books, 2006), 6.

5.　Ibid., 15.

6.　Ibid., 19.

7.　Ibid., 12.

8.　M. K. Weinberg, "Gender Differences in Emotional Expressivity and Self-Regulation during Early Infancy," *Developmental Psychology* 35, no. 1 (1999): 175–88.

9.　Brizendine, *The Female Brain*, 23.

three

WOMEN'S MINDS AND DISTORTED THINKING

I [Robert] was searching for something on the Internet one day and came across a chat room conversation. A man posted the following comment:

> Honest question, I don't know if women in other countries have the same problem, but I have never dated or met a woman in this country who did not suffer from low self-esteem, regardless of social status, family upbringing, accomplishments, etc.
>
> I have a coworker who is a pretty attractive girl in her early twenties. We went to the Iowa State Fair one night, and she told me that she was very self-conscious about her face (she has some very small acne scars) and her height (she is about 6'1"). She has no boyfriend and always complains about not being able to find one.
>
> I have never had a girlfriend who did not have low self-esteem or was happy with herself, what the hell is wrong with our women?

Now note the comments from women that responded immediately after the post: (actual comments!)

Comment #1

Just because you strike out getting American women with little to no self-esteem (all the time apparently) doesn't mean all American women have no self-esteem.

29

Comment #2

I'm willing to venture a guess that perhaps you can only get women with low self-esteem. Because I promise there are plenty of women out there that have plenty of confidence and self-esteem—we're just too smart to waste our time on guys like you.

Comment #3

I think just maybe the women with higher self-esteem just are not into dating fellows like you. I know many, many women, and most of them don't have a problem with self-esteem. Yes, they are interested in looking their best, but that is just about as far as they take it.

Comment #4

Like attracts like. Generally, we feel most comfortable around people we most resemble. If you see low self-esteem people all around you, ask yourself why you cultivate these types of relationships.[1]

Notice the apologetic nature of the responses from the women. This man's comments on this post were maybe a little harsh, but he obviously touched a raw nerve in these women. They immediately became defensive over his comments, becoming almost mean-spirited in their responses. Yet they needn't have—the man's observations were alarmingly valid.

Morty Lefkoe and his group of psychologists at the Lefkoe Institute have worked with over thirty thousand clients in counseling sessions over many years. Their conclusion is that it is quite rare to find a woman without low self-worth/self-esteem. Lefkoe said that these women sought counseling for an assortment of issues in their lives, but it almost always came down to the basic issue of self-worth.[2]

Could it be then that much of a woman's self-worth/self-esteem issues come from what she is telling herself about herself? Could it be that there is a fundamental flaw in her thinking? We think so— that goes for men and women alike. It is our thinking that gets us into trouble. Our aim in this chapter is to identify some of the most common thought processes or thought patterns that some might even label as distorted. Once identified—once we know the enemy—we can counter the attack by changing our thought processes. Let's look at a few:

All-or-None Thinking. Often in a woman's mind, everything seems black or white. There is no in-between; all things are absolute. This is true when it comes to moral agency, but not healthy when it comes to women's thoughts about themselves. Example: *"In my old neighborhood everyone was so super friendly. Nobody in this neighborhood likes me at all! I want to move."*

Notice the "everyone" and the "nobody"? It's all or none. Now if we asked the question "Is this really true? Can you think of any exceptions?" she would probably name a few. But seen in the light of her self-condemnatory style of thinking, the all-or-none, black-and-white thinking fits perfectly and feels comfortable to her. But the downside is that it digs her deeper into her self-made pit, and in the long run this way of thinking contributes to her social and spiritual downfall.

If she really looked into the matter more deeply, she might find that, because she is fairly new in her neighborhood, she is putting off a slight sense of aloofness, which has made her somewhat unapproachable by other women in the new area. Or she may recognize that because of her anxiety with the move, she has put in little to no effort to get to know her neighbors and that friendship is a two-way street. It would take a higher level of self-honesty for her to admit this. Once she was truly honest with herself, a completely new attitude would ensue. A better feeling returns, the distorted thinking of "all or none" disappears, and she starts making new relationships in the neighborhood. She may even find her new "BFF."

The Global Thinker. Example: "My seventh-grader got a D in math. I'm a total failure as a mother." This natural thought pattern suggests that one small part of your life touches every other part—usually negatively. It's the opposite of "compartmentalization." In essence it says, "If I fail in one small area of my life, that means I really am a failure overall."

Really?

Every woman can be set free from this type of thinking by using the truth. Is it *true* that because your son got a D on his report card that you are a total failure? Of course it isn't, but the natural thought patterns in you have you thinking that way. Later in this book we will be showing you exactly *how* to overcome this type of thinking if you choose to.

The Crystal Ball. We all do this, but women have it down to a science, and they use it constantly. We also call it "mind reading."

This is a seductive line of thinking.

It seems to be human nature to try to be a mind reader or fortune-teller. Mind reading is simply "knowing" how people are reacting to you—or "knowing" what their thoughts are about you.

Many women admit that they use their minds to immediately jump to conclusions despite the absence of any evidence that would support their conclusions. This can be very destructive. For example:

You are waiting in line in your car to pick up your daughter after school. Two women you know from the class are standing there talking to each other. As you get closer to the pick-up point, they both turn and look at you and wave, then turn back to each other and laugh. At this point you look into your crystal ball and *just know* for sure that they were talking about you. Your assumption, due to your uncanny ability to read peoples' minds correctly every time, tells you they were speaking negatively about you—even laughing about you! From that point on, you steer clear of them—never even saying hello in the school hallway or helping to be a recess monitor.

Now maybe it would have been better if you were an expert lip-reader instead of consummate mind reader. *Actually* they were talking about what they had put in their children's lunches that day, which made them both laugh. You thought it was all about you. Wrong.

And so you were "seduced" by yourself. If you watch carefully, you can catch yourself doing it all day long: with your best friend ("I saw the way she just looked at my shoes—she thinks they're out of style. *I'm* so out of style!"); your husband ("I know he thinks my hair is ugly but he won't say anything about it"); your new daughter-in-law ("I can tell she doesn't like my casserole; she hardly touched it").

Now let's look at the truth behind each of the above scenarios. Her best friend *was indeed* looking at her shoes, wondering if it would be too presumptuous to ask if she could borrow them. She's got an outfit that they'd go *perfectly* with. Ah yes, her husband *was* looking at her hair but was wondering how he's going to tell her that he forgot to pick up the dry cleaning on the way home. And your daughter-in-law is wondering when will be the right time to announce her pregnancy to the whole family—*and* the corresponding morning sickness.

Crystal-balling is also very useful for predicting the future. "I just know my book group presentation is going to flop. Nobody will listen." "I just know nobody is going to come to our couples' dinner party." "I just know I'm going to gain ten pounds through the Christmas season." Notice how each statement is preceded by "I just know"? *No you don't!* This type of thinking will only lead you down wrong pathways, and yet it happens all day long. The key is to recognize it right while it's happening and stop it in its tracks. We'll be teaching you how in the second half of this book.

The Double Standard. None of us likes a double standard. We cry foul if it's applied to us or our children. A double standard is defined as something that holds people accountable to different standards. The single standard then is a set of principles or rules that apply equally to everyone.

Do we do that to ourselves? All the time. Here's how: Mary, a mother of four wonderful children, struggles with critical thoughts about herself and constantly berates herself as a wife, mother, and friend. She came by it rightly—her own mother loved Mary, but she was often so critical of herself that it came naturally to Mary to likewise be self-critical. Mary found it almost impossible to think or say anything nice about herself and saw only personal flaws. She felt frumpy and was, according to her, about fifty pounds overweight. She felt worthless overall and had little reason in life to find any joy. She was sad. Not depressed, just sad.

Listening to Mary talk about herself was sad too. She was negative about most aspects of her life.

Here is where the double standard comes into play. Imagine Mary with her good friend Sarah. Her friend confides in her that she is really struggling right now. She is overweight. She feels frumpy. She has low feelings of self-worth. It's affecting her marriage and her relationship with her children. Listen in as Mary counsels Sarah on how she should look at herself (and see if you can detect the double standard in Mary's life):

Sarah: I don't know, Mary. I just feel so worthless sometimes.

Mary: Are you kidding me, Sarah? You are such a wonderful person. Whenever we're together, *I* compare myself to *you*. Your house is always so clean. Your kids are always so well behaved at church, and I wish I had naturally curly hair like yours! You always look so "put together."

Sarah: Really? Oh, Mary, thank you for the kind words. I just need someone to tell me once in a while that I matter.

Mary: Oh, Sarah, if you only knew. Jenny and I were just talking about you this morning on the phone, wishing we could cook the kind of meals you do for your family. Honestly, of all my friends, you are the kindest, most thoughtful person I know. You're always there for me. John even told me to hang out with you more because every time we've been together he says I seem to be happier!

Sarah: Stop! You're making me cry!

Can you see it? We hope you can. It's the double standard. Mary can "dish it out" to others; she can tell Sarah everything good and noble about Sarah—but when it comes time to recognizing what good there is in *herself*, she can't—or won't—do it. She builds all her friends and relatives up but chronically tears herself down. It's not fair, is it? It's a thought pattern that must be and can be eliminated. We don't like double standards when someone else treats us unfairly. But if we cannot recognize it in ourselves, we will be slaves to it forever.

The Discounter. We all discount to some degree, but some women are masters at this self-defeating behavior. For example, a friend at grocery store compliments you on your new hairstyle—and now you start discounting anything positive she says, "Oh, I can't do a thing with it! And she didn't cut it evenly." Your husband congratulates you for completing a literature class at the local junior college. Instead of saying, "Thanks, sweetheart. I really enjoyed the class, and I'd like to take another one sometime," you go right into discounting your good works, "Yeah, a lot of good it did me. I'm so behind on housework that I'll never have time to read another book! I don't know why I ever signed up for the class." You remember that, and the next time the opportunity comes to better yourself, you don't.

Always discounting the positive, never accepting your deep-down worth. And eventually you begin to believe the lie about yourself. Not that you set out to be hard on yourself—you had at one time all the optimism that life seemed to offer. But after your upbringing with parents that you could never please; the years of college, marriage, raising children; and some bouts of poor family economics, trials, and health issues, you got pretty badly beaten up by life. In that condition it's so much easier to believe the lies about yourself that the world would have you believe. Is it any wonder that whenever something good about you comes along, it's hard to believe?

The Perfectionist. Why is it so easy for us to forgive another of a simple error or mistake—but so terribly difficult to cut ourselves some slack? We do dumb things; we're human. There is a distinct difference between saying, "That was a stupid mistake," and "I'm so stupid." One is impersonal—the other is very personal. The former is commentary. The latter is condemnatory.

An honest mistake is to do something inappropriate or incorrect *with no evil intent.* These kinds of errors merit correction. But how do we judge ourselves? Rather harshly. Often a woman treats herself as though she committed some huge "sin" when it was an honest mistake. Again, it's the intent. For example, you forget your appointment at the dentist. The dentist's receptionist even called you the day before to remind you. They call you thirty minutes after the appointed time to reschedule you. You hang up and what are the first words out of your mouth? "I'm such an idiot!" or "Can't I do anything right?" You're a Blamer of Self. Would it be that hard to just get a grip on your thinking and say, "Okay—so I made an honest mistake. I'm not going to blow it out of proportion. Next time I'll set my cell phone alarm to remind me. Relax!"

THE TRICK

The "trick" with all these distortions in thinking is to examine your thoughts and immediately identify them. This requires practice. And practice makes perfect. In part two of this book you'll learn the techniques and receive the tools you'll need to start changing your thought habits—the kind of thinking that beats yourself up emotionally and mentally.

After interviewing many women over the years, we have come to the conclusion that women who *do* conquer their thought habits and learn to sift through the lies have much easier lives. *It's hard being so hard on yourselves.* Consider what the Bible counsels: "Ye shall know the truth, and the truth shall make you free" (John 8:32).

Here is a scenario we administered to six men and six women. We had them each read the following story. After reading it, they were instructed to respond if something similar were to happen to them. Here is the story:

> Today was an important day at work. You were the leader of a team that was making a presentation to the board of directors. You and the team had been working on this for several weeks. You were a little nervous but confident that you had done your homework and everything would go perfectly. All the research had been done. You were ready.
>
> You stood up to introduce your team to the board and then began your presentation. One of the board members sat there with his arms folded, a disgusted look on his face from the beginning. Frequently he would turn to the woman sitting next to him, say something, and she would nod in agreement.
>
> He finally raised his hand and began shooting holes in your

team's research. Frankly, he brought up points that you had never even considered. His accomplice next to him chimed in and added another valid point. You countered the best you could, but the chairman of the board finally stopped the bleeding by tabling the discussion and suggested that your team do its "due diligence" and attempt again in a few months. He was cordial, but you could tell that, despite anything you could say, or any research you had done, it was over. You sat down, lost in your thoughts.

We gave our six men and six women taking this test the following instructions: "Write down the immediate *feelings* and *thoughts* you would have in your mind if you were that person in the story."

Here are some of the comments from the men, which, we easily observed, were all very similar in nature:

- "We obviously didn't do our homework well enough."
- "We should have done better research. I wouldn't have let that happen if I were the team leader."
- "There's always someone sitting there that is the critic. They throw out all this negativity and say nothing constructive."
- "The next time we present, we'd have all our ducks lined up."
- "Okay. So we failed. It was probably due to lack of leadership on my part. I'd just step up to the plate and keep swinging until I hit the home run. Better preparation and research would do it."
- "That happens. I'd just have to reevaluate the processes we went through as a team. Sure, I'd be disappointed with how things went, but there's always a next time."
- "That guy sitting there is the kind of guy that wants to kill everyone else's ideas. You get used to that—so it's no big deal. I try not to let those kinds of people bother me."

Notice the theme that ran through their comments. Each one of them spoke in terms of "we" failed, "we didn't do our homework." They didn't take it very personally, but rather looked at it somewhat philosophically. "Next time" they'd do better. There was disappointment but no devastation.

Here are some of the comments the women wrote about how they would feel after such a meeting:

- "That would be mortifying. I can just see myself wilting in front of the whole group. I don't think I could get up in front of that group again. It would be just too painful."
- "I got a little anxiety just reading the story. If that really happened to me, I don't know how I'd react. I know I let the whole team down. I hate those kinds of situations."
- "I would really have to evaluate my performance. Why didn't I do more in-depth research? That would just devastate me if the chairman shut the whole thing down."
- "Arrrgh! That is so frightening. I would feel like my world just ended! I wouldn't have any confidence after that to do it again."
- "I can't stand those kinds of high-pressure meetings. I'm not cut out for that high-stress stuff."
- "I would just have to start all over. I didn't lead out. If it was my fault, I'd admit it and move on. When I make mistakes, I try to learn as much as I can from them."

Is there anything you notice particularly when you read those comments? Notice how the men did not personalize the whole incident. Most of them used "we" and not "I." The women personalized it by using "I" instead of "we." The women obviously felt more pain reading the scenario. Some of the men even blamed board members. Each of the women respondents seemed to blame themselves for the failure of the whole group.

Now, this is admittedly an extremely small sampling of people, but it does point out some big differences in how men and women think. If their beliefs about themselves are not true, not high or not robust, the thought patterns become predictive. Think back to the previous chapter where we talked about the childhood beliefs being so critical for the later years in a person's life. Think also about how a little girl is so much more tuned into feelings, facial expressions, and emotions than the boy. All these things accumulate to allow women to respond differently than men would. These thought patterns can be very destructive unless we have the tools to counter them.

MOTIVES

An experience we had with a women's focus group surprised us. This was a group of seven highly accomplished women, including a published author, a mother of nine children, and several business-women; some were single, some married, and two divorced. The topic of discussion turned to *why* all the women in that group had such self-deprecating thoughts about themselves daily.

Each of the women was contributing to the conversation when one of them quietly said, "It gives me *power*." The whole group turned to her as if to say, "Huh?"

> It gives me *power*, because when I'm at home and feeling really down on myself, I make it miserable on everyone else. The kids run and hide, and my husband will do *anything* at that point to pacify me. For a small moment during the day, I'm powerful. I hate myself when I do it. But it works. And at that point, *nobody* can talk me out of the fact that I'm a failure as a wife and mother. Sometimes I like it that way.

The focus group went silent for a bit. The other women were thinking about what she had said.

Then it occurred to us. This point was right in front of us, and we never saw it until she said it to the whole group: there was a *payoff*! She got something out of her self-deprecation, out of her momentary self-loathing. The other women in the group slowly nodded in agreement.

As researchers, it never occurred to us that there might be a powerful psychological payoff for the behavior so many women used on themselves: the self-critical comment about themselves muttered under their breath and the self-deprecating references about them being worthless. Why would a woman consistently do that to herself? Isn't it painful? Doesn't it make her life so much harder to go through? Couldn't she do it some easier way? Maybe not—if the payoff is big enough.

Put another way, we may ask ourselves if a woman punishes herself in her own mind, thinking she deserves to be treated subpar by herself, there may be some psychological benefit that even she may not be subconsciously aware of. In some way does it let her off the hook by not having to be accountable for her own thinking? Is it easier for her to be hard on herself, to beat herself up, than it is to be honest with herself and be responsible for her behavior? As Marianne Williamson said in our introduction,

> It is our light, not our darkness that most frightens us. We ask ourselves, Who am I to be brilliant, gorgeous, talented, fabulous? Actually, who are you not to be? You are a child of God. Your playing small does not serve the world. There is nothing enlightened about shrinking so that other people won't feel insecure around you.

That quotation is the truth about all of us, but if we have beliefs from our childhood that negate that, if we have old tapes playing in our heads that we are flawed, then there is a greater payoff by thinking small of ourselves than thinking large. We hold on to the past so we can escape accountability. We can fault peripheral situations or conditions. It's just plain easier—taking the path of emotional least resistance to disparage yourself is easier than it is to defend your own honor. It's such an inconvenience to uphold your dignity.

Strong words, we know, but we are trying to emotionally shake you enough to get you to realize that it doesn't have to be this way. You can stop the behavior—you can silence your inner critic.

We have talked in terms of the "payoff." For every payoff there is also a "trade-off." It may make you temporarily feel better in some perverse way when you are so self-critical, but there is a trade-off hiding somewhere inside the payoff. Each time you downgrade yourself, a little piece of your personal integrity is chipped away. A small chip here and there over the years and it's worn away, but anytime you take the payoff there is the trade-off. You select your future.

SELF-INFLICTED WOUNDS?

You may be asking this question: "Are you saying that I, as a woman, would intentionally 'hurt' myself by having negative thought about myself?" As much as it may sound a little harsh, yes, that is exactly what we are saying. Let us give you an example.

There is a behavioral phenomenon in the world today called *Deliberate Self-Harm* (DSH). The most common form of DSH is "cutting." Cutting is common among teens—some estimates run as high as 14 percent. Cutting may be seen on a teenager (especially girls) as knife cuts from the wrist to the elbow on one or both arms. Why in the world would people want to inflict injury to themselves, you ask?

Studies show several reason people give for engaging in DSH:

- To put an end to feeling bad
- To stop feelings of isolation or feeling empty inside
- To divert one's thinking from other issues
- To control anger
- To relieve stress or built-up anxiety

In other words, DSH can act as a coping mechanism. Other studies have been done, one in particular in 2006 by Chapman et al. In this study they postulated the "Experiential Avoidance Model of Self-Injury."

In this model they propose three reasons for DSH:

1. Distraction
2. Self-punishment
3. Release of endorphins (feel-good brain chemicals)[3]

All of these would then help them escape negative emotions about themselves. So these people who engage in physically harming themselves find a payoff. Maybe it's the release of feel-good hormones, or distraction, as stated above in Chapman's study. What is the trade-off? Permanent scars—or worse. Apparently the payoff to them is greater than the trade-off.

How does this then apply to our topic of low self-esteem? Would people actually mentally harm themselves by inducing self-deprecating thoughts? The answer, it seems, is yes. Could a woman sabotage her own self-worth by having recurring feelings of self-induced shame? Again, yes. Many girls who self-injure through cutting don't want to give it up because it is such a potent tool to alleviate negative feelings about themselves. They report feeling powerless without it.

Eckhart Tolle, in his book *The Power of Now,* states something very interesting in this regard: "Observe the peculiar pleasure you derive from being unhappy. Observe the compulsion to talk or think about it."[4]

We ask you then: do you, in some way, derive pleasure from being unhappy? Ask yourself truly, deep down inside. Does the hurting, the pain, or the suffering you are experiencing somehow feel good, even for the slightest moment? Is there something in your distorted thinking that makes you enjoy inflicting a little pain on yourself? Do you occasionally revel in feeling low, in feeling depressed, or in feeling isolated? Only you can answer these questions for yourself, but be honest. If you can be 100 percent honest with yourself, the second half of this book is meant for you.

As you can see, and as Chapman found, this causes more harm than it will ever solve.

We conclude this chapter with a few questions.

- Can you see that you might, at times, be guilty of some distorted thought patterns?
- What is "the trick" to conquering these distorted patterns? (See page 34.)
- Do you see the connection between the above-described self-injury model and what you might be doing with your thoughts?
- Do you derive some power or relief by being negative about yourself?
- Does it relieve you of any personal responsibility by taking the easy way out in your thinking negatively about yourself?

NOTES

1. "Why American Women Have Low Self-Esteem," Advameg, Inc., accessed May 7, 2013, http://www.city-data.com/forum/psychology/1070507-why-american-women-have-such-low-2.html.

2. "Re-Create Your Life: Transforming Yourself and Your World," Morty Lefkoe, 2013, accessed April 2013, http://www.mortylefkoe.com.

3.   A. Chapman, K. Gratz, and M. Brown, "Solving the Puzzle of deliberate Self-Harm: The Experimental Avoidance Model." *Behavior Research and Therapy*, (2006).

4.   Eckhart Tolle, *The Power of Now: A Guide to Spiritual Enlightenment*. (Canada: Namaste Publishing Inc., 1997), 42.

four

MARTYRS

What do Gandhi, Jesus Christ, Joan of Arc, and Martin Luther King all have in common? It is commonly held that they all died martyrs to a cause. Generally we define a martyr as one who chooses to suffer death rather than renounce religious principles. But we need to examine another more curious definition of the word: a martyr can also be anyone *who makes a great show of suffering in order to arouse sympathy or achieve some personal end.*

Admittedly, all of us have suffered at some time in our lives with what is called the "martyr complex." We have played the martyr to arouse sympathy or to try to make someone feel sorry for us—so we can control them. It may come across at first as being self-sacrificing, but in the end it is a scream for help. The classical martyrs such as Jesus Christ and Gandhi were happy people. People today with martyr complex are not happy. They feel helpless, and therefore must use this form of manipulation.

In an article titled "The Martyr Complex: The Poison That Kills Relationships," Jason Robillard wrote:

> People suffering from the martyr complex make unnecessary sacrifices at the expense of their own needs. Over the short term, this behavior appears to be helpful. . . .
>
> Over the long term, martyrs typically experience negative symptoms including psychological and physiological stress, resentment

that others aren't making the sacrifices they're making, and displaced anger at the object they're focusing on.[1]

Let's look at an example of how this plays out at home:

It was a warm, beautiful summer evening. Jessica had dinner prepared, the table set, and the kids all cleaned up for dad to arrive. Jason arrived right on time, gave Jessica a hug and a kiss, hugged each of the kids, and they all sat down to eat dinner. The meal was great, it was fun to talk, and generally mealtime was productive.

After the meal Jessica suggested to Jason that he take the kids out in the backyard and play with them for a while. "After all," she said, "the kids get to see you so little." Jason took them out and played on the lawn.

The kitchen window was open, looking out on the playing children, who were laughing, yelling, chasing, teasing, and having so much fun. Jessica was at the sink doing the dishes. As she looked out at her family playing together, feelings of resentment started building up. She began thinking that she should be out there too. Why is she always stuck in the house? The more she watched them, the angrier she got.

Then Jason yelled at her, "Honey, leave the dishes for a few minutes and come out and play with us! We'll come in and help with the dishes later."

Jessica waved them off. "No, you guys go ahead and keep playing. I have too much to do."

It may be true that she had a lot to do. But the key here is to recognize that she is not saying no to them because she has "too much" to do. She is doing it for herself. She derives that "peculiar pleasure" in suffering for the "greater cause." She is the victim; it's the ruined nobility. She also feels that it makes her look better in the eyes of her children and husband. Her "self-sacrifice" makes her more principled—or so she thinks. The funny thing is that she expects to be in some way recognized or rewarded for her sacrifice. But when offered, she refused. She also thought that this self-sacrifice might give her leverage or power over her husband and the older children later that night. It didn't work that way. Dad and the kids had fun; Mom was angry and resentful.

How did Jessica learn this behavior? Maybe she saw her mother doing the same thing as she grew up. Her father was somewhat of an austere, inflexible man, so she watched her mother constantly serving, but resenting, her husband. She always gave up what she wanted—maybe even lived her life through the lives of her husband or children. She too was a victim. Jessica learned from the best. Or maybe she read something that said it is better for her to always put others' needs before her own, so becoming the martyr was her own interpretation of how to do that. The satisfaction she experiences by being the temporary martyr may, for her, trump the pleasure she would get from playing in the backyard.

Can you see the payoff here? She may *think* that her husband and family see that she is "sacrificing" her own good for theirs, but in reality, all they see is an unhappy wife and mother, whose self-worth is low. It may make them feel guilty for a moment—they may wish they could do something for Mom-the-Victim—but then they go on playing in the backyards of their lives, and Mom is still the unhappy martyr. This is a no-win game for all, because the trade-off that always comes with the payoff of guilt, shame, and a perpetuation of the behavior being replicated in the children. Not a good trade-off at all.

So why would a sweet, loving mother like Jessica do that to herself? It causes her internal pain, and just like the teenage girls who cut themselves, she can cover pain from other things in her life or get the endorphin high from suffering momentarily. The payoff is short-lived. Let's not forget though: she is not doing this self-sacrifice for her family. She is doing it for herself.

The second half of this book will illustrate the tools and training you will need to get yourself out of this destructive habit.

NOTE

1. "The Martyr Complex: The Poison That Kills Relationships," Jason

Robillard, December 5, 2012, accessed June 5, 2013, http://sexpressionists. blogspot.com/2012/12/the-martyr-complex-poison-that-kills.html.

five

DESIRES AND DEFAULTS

I had a young lady in my office a little while ago, and we were talking about her health—in particular her weight. She stated that her social life was "not very good right now." She said she knew that if she could lose twenty-five pounds things would improve. So I asked her how she felt about her life in general. She said that in reality, she was miserable and that "life really stinks." I could tell it really revolved around her weight and appearance. She wasn't happy with herself.

"I really want to lose weight in the worst way," she kept saying. But this statement was followed up with the following actions: eating sugary foods at night while watching hours of television; going over to a friend's house and listening to "tunes"; clothes shopping/mall browsing; surfing the Internet and Facebooking.

Then she steps on the scale and says that she is just not able to lose weight at all. That is the ultimate cop-out. The truth is that she desires to do all those other things because she likes doing them *more* than she likes losing weight. But at the same time she is miserable. This is *not* about her weight; it's about her brain. If she is not taking action toward the thing she wants, she doesn't want it *enough*. Instead of her saying, "I want to lose weight," she should be truthful and say, "I want to lose weight to a point, but not *enough* to take action."

We know it's not really easy to do, but you have to be honest with yourself if you are going to end the misery or unhappiness in your life. Don't tell your spouse or best friend you really want to change if you are not willing to get up and do something about it. It is commonplace for many people to lie to themselves and others about how badly they want to change that they never look at the truth. Take the blindfold off; people usually do what they want to do, not what they have to do.

If we shine some light on our desires we find that everyone wants to grow in all areas of their lives: be more physically fit, earn more money, be emotionally perfectly stable—but not everyone wants those things to the same degree. If you don't take charge and *act,* you don't want it enough, and that's the truth about it.

- I want to lose twenty-five pounds, but I still eat junk food = I don't want to lose twenty-five pounds *enough.*
- I want to get better grades in school, but I spend my study time surfing the Internet = I don't want to get better grades *enough.*
- I want to make new friends, but I stay at home on weekend nights and watch TV = I don't want to make new friends *enough.*
- *I want to have better feelings about myself and I want to stop comparing myself to others,* but I make no mental effort to change my thinking = I don't want those things *enough.*

Surprisingly, this is *good* news. When you actually realize that you are not getting what you want as far as change in your life is concerned, it can be empowering. It helps you see why you are stuck where you are at this point in your life. Some people drive themselves crazy trying to figure out why they can't overcome procrastination, when it wasn't procrastination or even laziness to begin with. The simple fact is this: they didn't want it *enough.* The greatest desire will always win out. Always.

For example:

Karen: I don't know why I'm always so hard on myself. I really want to change how I feel about myself.

John: Have you decided what you can do about it?

Karen: I just don't have the time. I'm so busy.

John: Do you have ten minutes?

Karen: Yes.

John: Then you have enough time to at least look into what the alternatives are for you.

Karen: I guess I'm a little afraid of confronting the whole "I can't stand myself anymore" issues.

John: So you want to change yourself, but not as much as liking where you are right now with your feelings about yourself?

Karen: Yes, I guess so.

Aha! Finally the truth! Karen says she wants to change, but *not enough*. She likes the safety and comfort of the status quo—things just the way they are.

This is reminiscent of a story of two frogs hopping down a muddy road after a big rainstorm. All of a sudden, they both fall into a deep rut in the road caused by cars traveling in the mud. Both frogs jumped and jumped, and finally one of the frogs made it out of the rut, but the other frog didn't. "Keep trying!" said the frog to the one still in the rut. "I just can't do it—I can't make it. You go back to the pond without me."

So the one frog hopped back to the pond and crawled up on a lily pad and waited. About an hour later the other frog wearily crawled up on the lily pad.

"I thought you were never going to make it. What happened?"

"Well, I jumped and jumped and couldn't make it, and I gave up. But then along came a car down the same rut . . . and I *had* to get out!" Often it comes down to expediency: how much pain will I experience if I *don't* move? Does the pain of inaction then finally drive us to really want it badly enough?

Desire. Motivation. When you want to change the way you feel about yourself, when you want to stop believing the lies you tell yourself, when you want to stop comparing yourself to others *enough*, we can show you how in part two of this book. Pay particular attention to chapters 8, 10, and 11.

What is it really worth to you to not be plagued with the issue of low self-concept or low self-worth? For most of the women we have interviewed, it is a huge deal, but they don't have any idea how to tackle the problem. They are attacked multiple times per day. They constantly compare themselves to someone else's finest moments, someone else's greatest achievements, or someone else's only success, and never realize that they're not doing an apples-to-apples comparison. So after time, they give up having good, wholesome feelings about who they are. Instead, they have this chatter going on inside their heads, telling themselves multiple times per day that they are just not measuring up. Then they eventually begin to believe the lie. In the end, we know from our focus groups and interviews with women that living those lies is *not* worth it.

THE DEFAULT SETTING

Let us describe an analogy that everyone understands.

We have internal wiring in our hearts and brains. It's the way we are inside. To get out of the mental and emotional ruts, we have to ultimately change the internal wiring. Think of a computer: it has what is called a "default setting." The dictionary defines that as "Controls of a computer hardware or software (or of a device, equipment, or machine) as preset by its manufacturer. Some types of default settings may be altered or customized by the user."

Read carefully here, because it's talking about *you:* "Most programs have default settings which automatically provide certain information or guidelines or parameters for a certain program. *The computer automatically uses these settings unless directed otherwise.*" Likewise with the human brain, and this is critical to understand.

In a computer, this is a choice made by the program (when the user does not specify an alternative). The "program" (that which a woman thinks about herself) is, in many women, written by the *world* and not by the *truth*. This default setting must be changed, otherwise every time a woman is confronted with any situation in which she will compare herself, judge herself, evaluate her performance, or unconsciously compete with someone or something else, *she will go to the default setting,* which is determined by anything and anyone else but the truth.

This concept, we reiterate, is critical for you to understand. Your default settings are not true. Very often they are hideous, revolting self-concepts that somehow infiltrated your hardwiring and are a virus that needs to be eradicated. There are ways to do that, which we will discuss later in this book (see chapter 6), but be assured, you must recognize that your default settings are often wrong. It's the thinking you fall back on whenever you have a weak moment, or when you are standing at the edge of the self-contempt funnel, just about ready to jump in.

What is *your* default setting? When the storms come in your personal life (almost daily, we might add), do you revert back to your default setting, which may be made up of lies, untruths, and fictitious stories you have been telling yourself forever?

You *can* change that default setting. There is no reason not to. You are the only one standing in your way. No matter how many mind games you play with yourself, no matter how many times you believe you are the *exception,* you will at some time in your life have to confront your demons and deal with them. In part two of this book we will give you the tools that, *if* you will use them, can change your default setting and give you a new life of freedom from the kind of warped thinking that has been going on inside you maybe since you were a child. You (and your Higher Power) are the ultimate power over you.

YOUR BELIEF SYSTEM

Childhood is a wonderful time . . . for most of us. As stated earlier in this book, almost all of our beliefs about ourselves are established between the ages of one and eight. Notice we are saying they are *established.* That does *not* mean they are cast in stone and can never be changed. If you get nothing else out of this entire book, we hope you will catch the significance of this section on beliefs. It is critical.

Let's look at this logically for a moment: can you believe something that is not true? Of course you can. You can believe with all your heart that tomorrow morning the sun will not come up. Sure enough, up comes the sun, and your belief, based on the sun coming up, is proved inaccurate. So, you *can* believe a lie.

Hang with us here for a moment as we wax philosophical.

So all these beliefs you have formed about yourself in your childhood *could* be true, or they *could* be based on lies or on incorrect information. You can keep a belief in your head that you know is logically not true. That could have been in your head from when you were eight years old and your parents told you they were getting divorced and you heard them arguing about what they were going to do with you. From then on you may have had the belief that you were valueless or unwanted—a belief that you carry even today. But simply knowing where the beliefs come from is not powerful enough to remove them.

That belief will determine how you think and feel from then on. The question is this: who created that belief? Did your parents create it? No, you did. Their behavior may have caused it, but you created it. And you have maintained it all these years. So if *you* are the creator of your beliefs, then you are also the real architect of your life—because your beliefs form your life.

Remember, you cannot let your beliefs about yourself continue to ruin your life because most of them are not founded on the truth. They are merely beliefs founded on untruth. The problem is that these beliefs got into your head at a young age and stayed there and dictated thereafter how you think and feel about yourself. Can you see then that most of your negative belief patterns are founded on meaningless events that produced meaning in you?

So who originated your beliefs? You did. Who is the one that can reinterpret your beliefs? You are—no one else can do it for you—but you have to realize again that it was founded on misinterpretation, on lies, on untruths.

Can you go back to the "I" that existed before you misinterpreted what your parent said? We believe you can. Not through any mystical, transcendent journey, but simply by looking at and understanding the truth and repeating that truth in you enough that it takes over your thinking. Think of how many times throughout your life you repeated (either in your mind or verbally) to a spouse or close friend that ugly event when it seemed like neither of your parents wanted you. That became your default setting, which you go back to over and over again. Can default settings be changed? Of course they can be changed, and so can you, by reprogramming your thinking one day at a time.

You created your beliefs. You can change them. Those beliefs determine what you do and feel, so you can re-create your life by changing your beliefs. Those beliefs must become who you *were,* but they shouldn't define you now. Change the default setting.

DO YOU TALK TO YOURSELF?

Who talks to you more than you do? No one. We have found that people who have a low self-image tend to talk to themselves in demeaning ways. Sometimes they say these things only to themselves in their minds. Other times they might say these self-deprecating things out loud to others. It can become a default or habit—a habit that can be broken with the right training.

When we have told women to listen to what they are saying to themselves about themselves and then to write those not-so-good thoughts down, they are astounded at both the frequency and the severity of those thoughts. They are also astounded at the things that triggered those thoughts. When they reflect back on what triggered the negative feelings about themselves, they tend to be incredulous: they can hardly believe these thoughts when they look at them on the written page.

Self-deprecation is a mind-set. We use it to protect ourselves. We belittle ourselves or run ourselves down. "I can't believe I said that in the meeting today. I'm such an idiot." We may say this to our-selves first, knowing that someone else that was in that meeting either thought it or will tell us later, "I can't believe you said that in the meeting today. Did you really *mean* to say that?" It's your preemptive strike on yourself before someone else gets to you. Again, a protective device.

As explained earlier in this book, this type of thinking disparaging thoughts about ourselves often centers around our inability, as children, to measure up to our parents' expectations. Some of us never felt good enough back then, and we remember it now. So now you, as an adult, feel defective, even in some small way, and it continues to haunt and shame you. "I *should* have a sense of disgrace just for being myself. I have so little to offer anyone."

Let's clarify this a bit more by using a personal example. I [Robert] grew up in a somewhat dysfunctional home environment. Both of my parents were, unfortunately, alcoholics. They divorced. Both died from the effects of alcohol and smoking. I had three older sisters, two of whom had multiple divorces. Looking back, I told myself things like, "I must be broken too," and "I'll never really amount to much in life." I realized when I was a teen that many of my friends were growing up in great families with loving parents and wonderful childhoods. I just didn't happen to be in that group. When I was twenty-one years old, I knew I was somewhat "tweaked" and I recognized that my default setting was also "tweaked." So I made a decision at that time to change the default setting by changing my thinking. I could not change the past—nor did I really want to, because without having gone through what I did, I would not have had the inner strength to change the default. I did a lot of talking to myself. Reasoning with myself. Arguing with myself. I changed my tapes by changing my thinking through self-talk. I refused to believe the lies.

These faulty tapes of the thinking just described play over and over in our minds. These are misconceptions of the highest order. They are the lies we tell ourselves over and over throughout each day. After years of this thinking, we accept them as truth. Then fear sets in: the fear of total and complete inadequacy and we hear ourselves say, "I can't ever be good enough to satisfy anyone, therefore I never will deserve happiness or love or success in my life."

Psychologists talk about the greatest fear of all in the human mind. It's not spiders or snakes. It's not even public speaking. It is the fear of abandonment—of being left alone—even when we are surrounded by family and friends, because we think we are not normal or have no worth. Again, these are lies that we have carried from our youthful years. We believe in our own inadequacy.

How might that show up in our daily behavior? Let's look:

Beth, a single mom, works in an advertising agency as an administrative assistant. She has been working there for three years, but she has constant doubts about her ability to do the job correctly. At lunch with three other assistants, the conversation turns to Beth's new assignment to be the head of the new marketing project.

"Beth, are you so excited about the new project? That's quite the honor."

Beth replies, "I don't know why they picked me—you could do a much better job. I wish they hadn't asked me to do it. I'll probably mess it up and one of you will end up doing it anyway."

Translation: "I won't succeed on this project or in life. I don't feel good about myself. If I try to be as invisible as possible, maybe no one will notice how poorly I will do. I'm hoping though that if I belittle myself in front of you three, I will leave you with nothing to belittle me about—because I did it to myself first—so you won't have to say anything. Don't pay any attention to me, and certainly don't anticipate that I will accomplish anything."

Beth ultimately fears abandonment, so she abandons herself.

YOU GET TO CHOOSE

The following chapters are filled with helpful how-tos—how to change your thoughts and how to change your emotions. We'll even give you a few suggestions on how to change your chemistry. However, not one of those suggestions will make a significant difference in your life until you wrestle with this question:

Do you want to change?

One of the great secrets of life is to realize that we are each the result of our own individual choices. You are what you have chosen to be. This is not to say that other people and events have not influenced you, for better or for worse. That is undeniable. But by choosing how to react to and feel about the events in our lives, we retain control instead of being pushed into negative feelings. Both our greatest pains and our greatest joys are the direct result of our personal choices.

The world commonly uses the phrase, "free agency." We hear people say things like, "You can't make me do that. I have my free agency." Athletes use that term to describe a time when they get to choose the team for which they play. However, that phrase is misleading. There is such a thing as "agency" and there is "freedom," but they are not the same thing.

Agency is the power to make the choice. It is our will, our desire. Agency is the choice we make deep inside of us. Freedom is the power to act on those choices. Now here's the great secret: Freedom is the result of making correct choices. If we make dumb choices, we loose freedom and become captives to our choices.

For example, my local state government has granted me the freedom to drive a car because I have shown them a consistent pattern of making correct choices while behind the wheel. Those choices, my agency, have resulted in freedom. Now let's suppose that I began to make some poor choices, like driving too fast or carelessly. The government would then most likely give me a few warnings that if I continued to make those choices, I would lose my freedom to drive. If I persist with those poor choices, eventually my freedom would be lost.

At that moment, I might easily sit back, whine and complain about how horrible my state government is, and see myself as a victim. I could easily lead myself to believe that my misery is someone else's fault. "How dare they take away my license?" Thinking that way might relieve me of feeling responsible, but will also leave me feeling helpless, believing that my happiness is in the hands of someone else. But the truth is that the loss of freedom is due to *my* choices. I have no one to blame but myself. I chose to drive poorly.

The sooner we realize this truth and we begin to own our choices, the sooner we gain power. Your freedom is in your own hands. Your happiness is no one else's to control. If you are captive, if you have lost freedom; if you are unhappy, change your choices. Take ownership of those choices. You are as happy as you choose to be.

So, back to the question at hand. Do you choose to change? Do you want to be free of the harmful effects of Women's Weakness? Will you allow yourself to think things of you that you would never think of others? When a negative thought pops into your head, will you choose to control it, or will you allow it to stay? Do you choose to control your emotions? Will you stay out of the funnel?

We dare you to draw a line in the sand. To take a stand. To make a choice. This minute, choose to change. Choose to change the way you think and the way you feel. Enjoy the freedom that comes with that choice.

Part Two

The Solutions

Enough with the bad news! Men and women are broken; that's pretty clear. We both have a default setting that seems to be programmed into our DNA and that has caused no end of problems throughout our lives. Although many throw up their hands in disgust and say, "That's just the way I am; I can't change," our experience shows that is just not true. There *are* solutions; there *is* a cure. Both Men's Weakness and Women's Weakness can be overcome.

Part two of this book is designed to provide some tools that you can use to change your default setting. You *are* enough; you just need to silence that inner critic constantly telling you that you are not. These tools will help.

Not every tool will be of equal worth. Find the ones that work for you. Master them. Use them again and again until that default setting is reprogrammed. We have shared these tools with hundreds of women. Many of them have succeeded in changing their thoughts and their emotions. You can too. But remember one important key: These women did not *try*—they *trained*. There is a difference.

TRAINING VS. TRYING

To illustrate the difference between trying and training, consider the following illustration.

You entered a contest at your local gym. You put your name on a piece of paper and dropped it into a large container with hundreds of other women's names. The prize was $100,000, but there were two catches. First, your name had to be drawn. The drawing was two months away. Second, you had to bench-press one hundred pounds. The chance of your name being drawn was remote; nevertheless, the day of the big drawing arrives, a huge crowd had gathered there—each person anxiously waiting to see if their name would be drawn. The moment comes and sure enough, your name is magically chosen! You scream with delight and run up to the front to have your picture taken.

They announce your name again and also instruct that you have two weeks before the big lift: you have to bench-press one hundred pounds. The contest now overshadows all your thinking. Two weeks goes by, and you show up, dressed for the occasion. Your hair is perfect. You got your nails done just the day before. The press is there, and several hundred women to watch. The time comes. You lie down on the bench face up. Two rather muscular men slowly take the one-hundred-pound barbell off the stand and gradually lower it down to you. You take a firm grip and let it rest lightly upon your chest. The two men steadily let go of the barbell and the full weight of it rests upon you. Your moment is here; a hundred thousand dollars is riding on the next ten seconds. You have thought of hundreds of things that you will do with the money. You begin to exert all your best physical and mental effort to lift that barbell just twenty-four inches away from your body.

You couldn't even get it off your chest. It might as well have been three hundred pounds for that matter. You couldn't budge it. What went wrong? You *tried* as hard as you could. You mustered every last ounce of strength your arms and pectorals could utilize—but to no avail.

The two men finally lift the barbell off. A TV personality shoves a microphone in your face and asked how you felt. "I'm so disappointed. I *tried* as hard as I could. I guess it just wasn't meant to be."

The crowd disperses. You get in your car and make the painful drive home, lost in your thoughts about your failure.

In his book, *The Life You've Always Wanted*, author John Ortberg states:

> Trying hard can accomplish only so much. If you are serious about seizing this chance of a lifetime, you will have to enter into a life of training. You must arrange your life around certain practices that will enable you to do what you cannot do now by willpower alone. When it comes to [lifting a hundred pounds], you must train, not merely try.[1]

This is the guiding principle for the next sections of this book; there is an enormous difference between just *trying* your hardest to change your thinking and really *training* to make changes in your mind.

To change your default settings you must train.

Part two of this book is your training manual. If you merely read the pages, you are trying. If you use the tools daily and consistently, you are training. One works; one doesn't. Both require some effort. One will pay huge dividends; the other won't. Your future is up to you. The exciting part is that the training is fun, and payoffs start right away. You *can* lift that one hundred pounds—but only if you *train*.

These default settings we keep talking about are actually the neural pathways in the brain. Every memory or experience we have ever had is still in our brain. These memories are literally etched into the crevices in that gray matter. Researchers have actually demonstrated this by inserting electrical probes into certain areas of the brain. They then sent a tiny amount of electricity along that probe and into the brain tissue, which elicited a memory from that person's childhood that they hadn't thought of for forty years! But it was still in there. When you think of the childhood trauma and distress each of us may have gone through, even with loving, well-meaning parents, you can begin to understand how much "baggage" we have stored away in our brains. At the right moment, they come out like some little gremlin to haunt us.

The good news is by the time you reach maturity, the neural pathways (or memory grooves) are pretty well established in the brain. However, the brain can be reconfigured. In brain research it's called *neuroplasticity*. Just like a piece of metal is hard, the brain is nevertheless malleable, pliable, and bendable. You can turn it in to something else. You can change your thinking through training methods such as self-observation and self-inquiry and thus gain more control over your self-worth. If you think you are hopelessly chained to thinking poorly about yourself, you are wrong. Science says you are wrong. Research proves you are wrong, and most assuredly, your conscience, deep down inside, tells you that you are *more* than enough.

Let us now show you how—with the tools of change.

NOTE

1. John Ortberg, *The Life You've Always Wanted* (Grand Rapids, MI: Aondervan Publishing, 1997, 2002), 46.

six

THE TOOLS OF CHANGE

We spent the first half of this book describing (in somewhat painful detail) the problems that women face with their thinking. We hope that by now you see the enemy. The enemy is your thinking—thought patterns that have been with you most of your life. They are, in major and minor ways, destroying your peace of mind.

Now we are switching gears in a big way. We are heading into the "tools" part of the book. We will lay out for you the most successful tools people have used to get themselves out of the "funnel" of improper thoughts about themselves.

A tool is defined as a "device for doing work." Yes, we can describe the tools, but you will have to do the work. It will not be much physical work; it will be mental exertion, and we have seen it work time and time again when people will do that work. As described previously, you must not just try, you must train, and we'll show you how.

YOUR NEW TOOL

Imagine that you are sitting at home and the doorbell rings. Sitting on your porch is a large brown package. You bring it in and open it. Inside you find a strange-looking implement of some kind. You honestly have no idea what it is. In a way it looks like a small wooden box with a blade attached to the top. You scratch your head. What in the world? No instructions came with it. It has some moving parts to it. "Must be something for the kitchen, since it has a blade," you muse.

The box is big enough maybe to put a softball in it. It has little holes in the bottom and a little bowl hidden below that. You're stumped.

You decide to find out exactly what it is in the only way a true "techie" would: you take a picture of it with your cell phone and post it on the Internet with the question: "Does anyone out there know what this gizmo is? Help!"

Within minutes, you start getting answers. Turns out it's a "coconut splitter." You balance a coconut on the top of the box and jam the blade down onto it. The liquid then drains to the bottom bowl. Now you have two halves. You can then balance a half piece on the top and split it.

Just what you needed, right?

Dutifully, the next time you go to the store, you buy a couple of coconuts. You come home, set up the gizmo, and jam that blade down on top of the coconut. The coconut is sent flying through the air, across your kitchen and smacks the wall, still intact.

You go back to the Internet and ask the question, "How in the heck do you use a coconut splitter?"

Answers come back: "It's all a matter of balance." "It takes a lot of practice and patience." "Rookies will be frustrated." "It's all about how you put the coconut on the box." "If the coconut is exactly vertical, it won't fly out."

By now you're thinking, "What sadistic person sent this to me?" But you're not a quitter. You buy a few more coconuts and try it again. This time you stopped the coconut from hitting the wall because you put a cardboard box on the counter . . . just in case.

By the sixth coconut, you have it down to a science. It's really a great tool—you just had to learn how to use it. You even read up on how good coconuts are for you and your kids. You start using the splitter daily. It's easy.

We hope you get the point of the coconut splitter story. We are now giving you a very powerful tool to control your thinking, a tool to reset your default setting. But, like the splitter, you won't really know how to use it unless you actually start practicing or training with the tool. You may have a few coconuts "hit the wall" but with time, you will be able to use these tools automatically, without thinking. That is the key: they must become automatic—a reflex. As soon as you are triggered in any way, you automatically use these tools. Let's look at your first and most powerful tool—one that will serve you well for the rest of your lives. Once you learn it and "get it down," teach the use of the tool to your children or friends so they don't have to go through what you have.

CSG

This tool comes in three parts: Confront, Scan, and Go. Just memorize them in that order, because you will use this over and over again.

In chapter 8 we will explain in more detail the principle of "Stimulus/Response." In a nutshell, it means that between every stimulus (whatever it is that triggers you) and response (however you choose to respond to that stimulus) is a space of time. That space of time is exactly where you use this tool, CSG. You can train yourself to insert CSG after every stimulus in your life that triggers you to step into the funnel of low self-worth, low self-esteem, self-deprecation, or self-hatred. The first challenge, however, is to always notice the trigger. Recognize when you experience those feelings of standing at the edge of the funnel and you feel ready to jump in. Maybe the trigger at first causes an immediate feeling of hopelessness Maybe anger. Maybe a strange sensation, the proverbial "pit in the stomach" and you just know what's coming next. Whatever form it takes, it's always a thought first. You catch it before it ever goes from electrical to chemical. Then you . . .

Confront

Many people think that when you have a bad thought about your-self, or a trigger, you should shun it, put it out of your mind, run from it, avoid it, ignore it, or even deny its existence. Wrong! Nothing could be further from the truth. It may seem a little counter-intuitive, but to stop unwanted thoughts, you absolutely must concentrate on them. If you avoid or ignore them, they will swallow you up sooner or later—probably sooner. You need to confront them straight-up. Stare them in the face. Acknowledge them immediately. Challenge them. Meet them head on with the intent of defying them. This is the only way to deal with them. Stop whatever you are doing and confront when the stimulus hits you.

One of the best ways to confront a trigger is to talk to it. Sound strange? Maybe, but we have found that confrontation is best done by acknowledging the trigger by actually treating it as a living entity. Here's an example:

> Emma was walking through the mall and browsing the windows of the clothing stores. She was supposed to meet her husband and she had about ten minutes to kill. She walked past a lingerie store and looked at some of the clothing displayed in the window. Then she caught her reflection in a full-length mirror positioned directly behind a mannequin. As she compared her figure to what she saw dis-played in the window, she felt that old feeling immediately starting to go to her stomach. She had been triggered through comparing. Before she knew about CSG, she would have jumped into the funnel of low self-worth without even questioning it. Listen to her thinking as she effectively confronts the gremlins:
>
> "Well, here you are again, right in front of me. I see exactly what you're doing, and it's not going to work this time. You're trying to trigger me, and I'm on to you now. I'm starin' you down. I defy you to get me! I'm smarter than you are. I know your game, and I will not lose. I've played your game in the past, but that's not me anymore."

That, simply put, is confrontation. We see it work over and over again in women who will practice it. Training. Not trying. Every time you get triggered, you confront before it goes from the thought to the feeling, or from electrical to chemical. This is a huge factor. It is referred to as "pattern interrupt." You are literally interrupting your thinking on the spot by confrontation, by acknowledging that you have been triggered and not letting it "go chemical."

Consider the scenario of a woman driving down the street at the speed limit. Another vehicle driven by a "little old lady" pulls out in front of her, causing the first woman to have to slow down to a crawl. How would confrontation look in this case? For most of us this is a huge trigger: as soon as you see the car pulling out, you automatically confront it before you "lose your cool" (incidentally, the phrase *lose your cool* is just another way of saying that you've gone from electrical to chemical).

"Aha! There's the first trigger this morning! I see what is going on here. No, you're not going to get me. I'm not chemical here. That little lady in the car was put in my path just to test me. I'm fine. I'm in control. It's a great day!"

Does this sound Pollyanna-ish? It's not at all. Pattern interrupt has been used by psychologists for years to help people control the faulty thought patterns established in their lives. We have used this tool with many people, and as simplistic as it sounds, it works every time it's used. But we are not going to stop there. There is more to CSG than just the *C*.

Scan

The *S* in CSG stands for "Scan." This is a critical component of changing your thinking about yourself. Let's look at a comment a woman in a focus group said she makes about herself whenever she "messes up": "I'm so pathetic." She said that thought creeps into her mind whenever she doesn't meet someone else's expectations, whenever she makes a mistake, or whenever she just feels blue. (So if she's human like the rest of us, that's probably a considerable amount of time each day.) If she will learn the following self-scan process, and use it as a tool, she will have a most powerful weapon in her arsenal to combat and destroy the "I'm so pathetic" thinking every time she feels that thought coming on.

THE BIG THREE QUESTIONS OF SELF-SCANNING

As you use this tool, you will begin to escape most of those moments in your life when the self-doubt, the self-contempt, and the insecurities that follow you around constantly rob you of your peace. You must ask yourself three self-scan questions (that means that you need to memorize these three questions) at the very moment the thoughts start invading your mind. First, you confront the thoughts as illustrated above, and then you scan yourself with the following questions:

1. *Is what I am telling myself right now really true or is there a lie in there somewhere?*
2. *What am I fearing right now?*
3. *Right now—am I heading into darkness or into light?*

We call these "The Big Three" questions. You must challenge your thinking with them when you are standing at the edge of the self-hatred funnel, getting ready to jump in. All honesty begins with self-honesty.

To recall them more easily, remember three words:

True—Fear—Light

Let us examine each question to show the power in them.

1. Is what I am telling myself right now really true or is there a lie in there somewhere?

Let's face it: we lie a lot to ourselves. The key word in this question is *really*. It implies reality, things as they *really* are—not how we imagine them to be, or how we think other people are thinking. It's the truth, and the truth is sometimes inconvenient to confront.

In our focus groups we have had women think about a particular dark thought they have about themselves—a pernicious and persistent negative thought pattern that keeps showing up (aka a "gremlin"). Then we ask them, "Okay, now that you have brought up that thought and are holding it in your mind, answer this question: 'Is what you are telling yourself right now *really* true on every level all of the time in your life, or is there a lie in there somewhere?'"

The responses are incredibly enlightening. In virtually every case, after arguing and explaining, each woman would eventually admit that what she was telling herself was not really true. A little lie was lurking somewhere beneath, a lie that they believe in their weakest moments. It's been with them so long, and they have repeated it enough in their heads, that they ended up believing it, even though it's not *really* true.

To illustrate, imagine yourself at work sitting behind your desk when your boss comes in. He throws a report on your desk and briskly says, "This is not at all what I wanted. Please do it over." He turns around and walks out, saying nothing else. Your first reaction is, "He can be such a jerk sometimes." But as your default setting kicks in, you immediately start to beat yourself up, listening to your critical inner voice saying, "It seems like nothing I do is ever good enough. I ought to just quit this job. Lisa should have my job—she's so much more qualified. I just don't have what it takes in so many things."

If we went back now and examined each of her self-critical statements and ask if *absolutely everything* she just told herself about herself is 100 percent true, we would find that it is not. Lies are lurking in there. "Nothing I do is ever good enough." That is not true; many things she does every day are good enough. But because she is in a self-deprecating mode at the moment, she refuses to see any good in herself. "I just don't have what it takes." Really? What does it "take"? That is an overgeneralization and is not true.

Loving What Is author and lecturer Byron Katie goes in to great depth with this type of self-inquiry. She suggests some of the same type of questioning:

> Is your problem true? Can you really know it's true? Can you find a peaceful reason to believe it? Who would you be without it?

That is the most intriguing question of all, isn't it? Who would you be without these thought patterns or old tapes running around in your head? Answer: you would be free.

2. *What am I fearing right now?*

The answer to this simple question, for many women, turns out to be terrifying at first. Again, in our focus groups and interviews with women, when we ask them this question as a follow-up to the first question (the truth), we have seen truth dawning on them sometimes for the first time in their lives. "What do you mean 'What am I fearing right now'?" they'll ask. "I'm not fearing anything."

"Oh, okay. Let's go back to what you wrote on that paper. It says you have these sabotaging thoughts about yourself and your relationship with your husband. Is that correct?"

"Yes."

"Tell us about that. Why do you think you continue to belittle and downgrade yourself because of your relationship with him?"

"I don't know. I guess it's my weight."

"Your weight?"

"Yeah. I know he looks at me and is disgusted with my weight."

"He's told you that?"

"I know that's what he's thinking. I can see it in his face."

"Has he come right out and said that?"

"Well, no—he's too nice to say what he's thinking."

"So you can read his mind perfectly every time?"

"Well, no, it's just that I'm ashamed."

"So it's not your husband, really?"

"No, it's me. I'm just afraid that someday he'll leave me, or that because of my weight I'm going to die young or something."

"You used the term 'afraid.' So there is fear involved in how you are treating yourself?"

"Yeah, I guess there really is, when you put it that way."

"What's your greatest fear?"

"I suppose being alone. Okay, this is really scary!"

"Do you really think your husband or your children would leave you?"

"No. I know they never would."

Identifying the underlying fear is critically important in

overcoming the low self-worth issue, because in almost all cases, it's a phantom fear, as illustrated in the conversation above. It's imagined—nevertheless it's real at that moment in your life until it's confronted and debunked. Note the acronym:

F.E.A.R. = False Evidence Appearing Real

CASE STUDY

Sydney, one of our focus group attendees, reported this illuminating experience in her life:

> I was invited to attend a jewelry party at a neighbor's house one evening. I called another neighbor and asked her if she was going to it. She was, so we decided to show up together. I guess there's strength in numbers, because I always feel so self-conscious going to something like that by myself.
>
> The evening arrived. I wore a cute spring outfit with my new shoes. Not overdressed, but stylish. I picked my friend up, and we arrived just after it started. There was a fun group of women there and I felt safe.
>
> About fifteen minutes later, a former member of the neighborhood showed up. She had moved several years ago, and now I hardly recognized her. She had lost weight, had a great tan, and looked like she was in great shape. She even changed her hair color and style. We all took notice.
>
> Everyone at the party swarmed around her to say hello. I joined the group. When she looked at me she barely acknowledged me, but was friendly to everyone else. I honestly felt snubbed. What had I done to her? So there I stood standing on the outside of the circle, not included. Not part of the 'in group.'
>
> Then it started—those thoughts about myself. *I'm a nobody. I'm a loser. I don't count. I don't have any real friends. What am I doing here, anyway? I just want to leave, now! She sure looks great. She must be a size 2. What has she been doing? I think I'll color my hair like that . . .* What am I doing? Here I am an adult, and I feel like I'm back in junior high at a sleepover, getting left out again.
>
> And then I remembered the time that I had been in your focus

group when we talked about that Self-Scan thing you taught us and the three questions we are to ask ourselves. I was in such a weak, vulnerable place that it scared me so much I thought about doing what you told us to do. So I asked myself to scan my thoughts *right then* to see if what I was telling myself about myself was true. It was as if a bolt of lighten hit me right in my heart as the words came into my mind "You are lying to yourself." It was so clear it almost took my breath away.

The longer I stood there looking at the group, the more I did the little Self Scan process. I could see that I was mind reading all of the women in the whole room. *I* wasn't *being* snubbed; I was snubbing *them*! I was blaming them for my thoughts about myself—and those thoughts weren't even true! Talk about going into darkness! I was going there fast.

And when I asked the second question, what am I fearing right now, I almost burst out laughing! I couldn't believe I was fearful of what some former member of our neighborhood was going to do to me. Nothing! Nothing at all! And I was blaming her? I couldn't believe my thoughts.

Now I use your Self-Scan all the time to get myself out of tight spots. Sometimes at the very first sensation I get of comparing myself or getting down on myself, I just start self-scanning and I pull myself out of those dark places. Thank you so much for telling us about it that night in the focus group.   —*Sydney M.*

3. Right now—am I heading into darkness or into light?

- In many of our focus groups with women, we have noticed a word coming up so often that we had to address the issue. The word is *darkness*. Women told us that when they are feeling themselves get "sucked into the funnel" of self-condemning they also felt a darkness surrounding them. It can be, they say, a real sensation. Our point here is this: if they can feel themselves slipping into darkness and recognize that sensation, they can sometime instantly turn it around and head back into the light.

- The problem is with the recognition. Most of the women told us that they couldn't see or feel it coming. So we had them start asking the question every time: "Right now, am I heading into darkness or into the light?" If they can handle the truth, then they'll admit right then and there that they are indeed slipping into the darkness funnel. With one brief question, they can turn it around.

- Light is so much more comfortable than darkness.

"SCAN" YOURSELF

Experience shows us that women who practice the Self-Scan can make tremendous strides in overcoming Women's Weakness. Whenever you are triggered or feel the slightest anxiety or uneasiness sneaking into your mind or whenever you feel your emotions trembling in any way or sense your low self-esteem shouting out in any way, try to step off somewhere mentally and scan yourself. It can be immensely helpful in all situations at anytime. At that moment you quickly evaluate what the truth of the situation is, and what the honest course we should take is—regardless of whether it is challenging or not.

It is not easy to catch yourself in the act, but the more you do it the more natural it becomes. It will be a battle of the mind until it becomes automatic in your thinking. If, however, you seek peace of mind, it is necessary to control your mind. The Self-Scan is how to do it, and as often as you use it, it will work. Our feedback from women who have tried it is overwhelmingly positive.

To summarize: the *S* in CSG stands for Self-Scan. It has three questions you ask yourself:

1. Is what I am telling myself right now really true?
2. What am I fearing right now?
3. Am I heading into darkness by what I am telling myself right now?

GO

The *G* in CSG stands for **Go**. That's it. Just plain old go. What do we mean by that?

Another powerful pattern interrupt, it must be included if you are to not jump into the funnel. After you have adequately confronted your thoughts (step 1) and after you have scanned and asked yourself The Big Three (step 2), you now *go*, moving into some type of action.

You do something right then and there. You connect with someone or something. For instance: you compliment someone; you smile (even at yourself in the mirror—or even without a mirror); you do something kind. The point is you are attaching yourself to someone or something else for a moment, just long enough to achieve the pattern interrupt, and get the old tapes out of the way so you can see the truth of what is currently happening in your mind.

Maybe you do something nice for a friend. Maybe you merely say out loud to yourself, "I feel wonderful. I feel happy. I am free from my old self." You are reaching outside of yourself. You are creating an instant "mini bond" to get outside your own thinking. Maybe you start naming things you are grateful for. Maybe you call your best friend and compliment her or thank her for something. Maybe you do a quick, kind deed, like making your son's bed, even though he knows he is supposed to do it as part of his daily chores. Or you send a quick email to your daughter away at college. You compliment a fellow worker—nothing big, just a kind word.

You'll be amazed at how much the word *go* can break the pattern. But this is work! It's part of the training we have talked about. If you merely just "try" to go, you will fail in the long run. You must exert yourself mentally to actually go into some sort of mini action. Training, not trying. You must do this over and over again in your head until it becomes automatic. Just like a moth at night is attracted to light, all humans are attracted to "light." We tend to dislike darkness and are drawn to light metaphorically. Look at it this way:

$$Darkness \leftarrow You \rightarrow Light$$

At any one moment you are either going into the light or going into darkness. You are not stagnant, because you are always consciously thinking (unless you are asleep). Each thought leads to some destination. Religious leader David O. McKay put it this way:

> The thought in your mind at this moment is contributing, however

infinitesimally, almost imperceptibly to the shaping of your soul, even to the lineaments of your countenance. . . . even passing and idle thoughts leave their impression.[1]

The word *go* encompasses the movement of going from darkness into light. When we degrade ourselves, belittle ourselves, or have bad thoughts about ourselves to any degree, we are moving into darkness, and we know, deep down inside, that it does not feel good, even though we may get some kind of temporary payoff for it. The further we go into darkness, the more hopeless we become. Going into the light is marvelous. It's freeing, liberating, and almost intoxicating. Here's an example:

My wife sent me [Bryce] to Costco with a long list of things to get. It was the day before the Fourth of July. I got there at 11:00 a.m. thinking I would "beat the crowd." Ha! The cars were lined up back to the street. I could barely get in the parking lot. I had my two young daughters with me. I guided the car down one aisle. No luck. Down another aisle. No luck again. I turned down a third aisle and noticed a couple walking to their car. I pulled up to them, rolled down my window, and asked them if they were leaving.

"Yes. We're in that white SUV there on the left." This was great. I pulled forward a little and put my blinker on so people would be aware of what I was doing. As I was patiently waiting, I saw another car coming from the opposite direction, also hunting a parking spot.

I could see immediately what was happening. I said out loud, "If those people take my spot when they can see darn well that I'm sitting here waiting for that spot . . ." My two wide-eyed little girls in the backseat were bracing for the worst.

As the SUV backed out toward me, the other car quickly pulled into the space.

Stop the story right here. What are you thinking right now? Has something similar happened to you? Probably. As I sat there seeing what was happening, I could literally feel myself going into darkness. My anger was increasing. I was taking my agency, my freedom, and rolling it up into a nice, neat package, and throwing at the car that "stole" *my* parking place. I was in darkness. It didn't feel good to me, nor did it feel good to those two little ones in the backseat.

The fortunate fact is I had been in training. I had been practicing catching myself going into darkness and consciously retrieving myself and going back into the light.

The story continues: I rolled down my window, ready to say something undoubtedly rude, but I caught myself. I knew by the looks on their faces as they got out of the car that *they* knew they had stolen my place. As they walked by my window, I smiled, nodded, and said, "How ya doin'?"

I was victorious! Not over them—over myself. I had won a private battle inside my mind by hurrying out of darkness and back into the light. My daughters could hardly believe what had happened.

"Dad? Weren't you mad?"

"Well, for a moment I was—but I didn't want those two people ruining my whole day. It's not worth it. I'm over it."

Do you think two little girls learned something from Dad that day? I hope so, but I know I had my private victory. I was liberated from the tyranny of my own thinking.

Go—a simple word to get you back into the light. Move. Do something. Act. Don't just sit there when the negative self-thoughts attack. When you have a self-esteem attack, you move right into CSG. Have you memorized it?

PUTTING IT ALL TOGETHER

You can see by now that when we talk to ourselves negatively—whether or not the statements are true—they still become the dogma that we live by. That's precisely why we need to have the tool CSG. Now let's go through a new scenario using your "old way" and then again using your new way of CSG. Here's the setup:

It's Tuesday night and you head over to the junior high for parent-teacher conferences. Your husband was out of town, so you're going it alone. Your thirteen-year-old son, Brady, is doing well in school. He makes you proud.

You have a great visit with his English teacher. All assignments completed, and mostly A's and a couple of B's on his tests. What more could a parent ask for?

Biology class was the same. The teacher says Brady seems to be one of the brightest kids in his class. You're beaming by this time.

You advance to his Algebra II class. You sit down and give your student's name to the teacher, Mrs. Albright. She immediately says, "Ah, yes, Brady. You do know that Brady is flunking this class, don't you?"

You're stunned. "Excuse me? Flunking? What do you mean?"

"I mean he's performing very poorly. His assignments aren't coming in, and the last three tests he flunked. Is everything okay at home?"

A little defensive now, you reply, "*Of course* everything is okay at home. I'm just a little bit surprised at this news. Brady's a good kid."

A little impatiently, with the "that's what they all say" look on her face, Mrs. Albright asks, "Is there anyone at home that could help him with factoring polynomials and quadratic equations. You *do* know how to factor, *don't you?*"

"Uhh, yeah, I can handle that, and so can my husband." You're thinking "Polynomials? Factoring? And what was that other word she used?"

As you walk to your car, your mind is filled with questions. Those questions, however, are not centered on Brady. They are centered on you. Here's what they sound like:

"What kind of a mother am I?"

"Why didn't I read to him more when he was little?"

"*I never did* understand algebra. No wonder Brady is flunking."

"Why didn't my mom and dad help me more with math? Dad always did like Sarah more that he liked me."

"This is a joke. I'm a fraud as a parent. Why can't I do anything right?"

"Why hasn't Brady said anything about this? Am I *that* unapproachable as a parent?"

"We're just going to have to get him a tutor. I can't do this and Ron is never home to help. If I didn't have to work, I could help

Brady. Who am I trying to kid? I've got a master's degree in psychology, not math! Look where it's getting me."

"Is there anything going right in my life? My kid is flunking out of school. What are the other parents going to think?"

"Poor Brady. He must be miserable carrying this around with him all the time. I haven't even asked him how his classes were going. Is it that I just don't care? Am I too tired to care? But how could I keep up with all that? Look at me: my hair is ugly, my kids are flunking out of school, and I'm twenty pounds overweight!"

You sit in you car in the parking lot, in the dark, and cry. A total failure.

That's how *you* see it. You haven't done any reality check yet to see if there is any legitimacy to your conclusions.

Notice how the situation has enlarged itself in her mind to encompass far more than the original situation deserved?

Now let's go back and see what CSG can do to help you out of this darkness and back into the light.

FIGHTING BACK WITH CSG

Let's revisit this scenario and each of the statements, one by one and see how you can counteract this thinking with CSG:

As you are walking to your car, your mind is filled with questions. Those questions, however, are not centered on Brady. They are centered on you. Here's what they sound like:

"What kind of a mother am I?"

[At that very moment you catch yourself and confront that thought: "Okay. This is a tough situation. Brady is flunking math. My old thinking would make me question my mothering capabilities, but I see what's happening right now. I hear my old tapes playing, but I am not going to let myself get triggered. I'm facing this one head on."]

Now that you have confronted the thoughts, you shift into scanning yourself:

[Okay, let's see. Self-scan. The first question is this—is what I am telling myself right now the truth or is there some kind of a lie in thinking that I'm a lousy mother. Well, actually, I know deep down inside that I am *not a lousy mother*. I know that I have made some mistakes along the way, but I have three great children and I would be lying if I said I wasn't a good mom. All right, now what's the next question? Oh yeah, what am I fearing right now? Uh, I fear he will flunk the math class. I fear that other parents I know will think less of me as a mother. Wait a minute—what do I care about other parents? It's none of their business. I care about Brady. Okay, what else do I fear here . . . Maybe that people will make fun of Brady if they find out he is flunking math. Really? That's stupid—everyone loves Brady. Okay, these fears aren't actually real, are they? All right then, I can see that I'm just playing head games with myself. Next question? Um, oh yeah, am I heading into the darkness or into the light? Duh, that's pretty obvious by now. Thinking I'm not a good mom doesn't do me a bit of good. If I think that about myself, that's sure not going to help Brady—or me! Yep, I was going into darkness, but now I'm turning it around. I like being in the light. It feels so much better!]

Do you see how this works? Good, but we are not done yet, are we? Now that you know you were headed toward darkness, you have to head toward the light with the *G. Go!* You are sitting in your car in the school parking lot. Now you have to do something. You whip out your cell phone and send a quick text to your best friend that reads, "Lisa, just a note to say I really appreciate our friendship. Thanks for being the person you are."

By now, you're not even close to the edge of the funnel. You are back in the light, thinking non-fearful thoughts. Stimulus—Response. What did you do with that space in between those two words? Did you allow the electric impulses to become chemical and spill out all over your body? No, you used CSG effectively and it worked. Later that night you even got a phone call from your friend Lisa saying that that text came at just the right time, because she'd had a bad day and you turned it around for her. Hooray for you!

Now you can look at the other comments you made about yourself on the way to your car, and you can see how CSG can help each one of them. Let's do one more to help you get the hang of it.

"We're just going to have to get him a tutor. I can't do this and Ron is never home to help. If I didn't have to work, I could help Brady. Who am I trying to kid? I've got a master's degree in psychology, not math! Look where it's getting me."

Confront:

[Ah yes, I'm just getting ready to jump with both feet into the funnel. Nope. Stop right here. I feel it. I'm going into darkness right now as I'm walking to the car. Stop it!]

Scan:

[Am I telling the truth right now or is there a lie hidden here? Yep, Brady needs a tutor. As a matter of fact, Sarah next door is a straight-A student and *she* has a tutor. What's the big deal? Realistically neither Ron nor I have the time to do this or maybe the know-how. So what? Of course I have a brain—but probably not for factoring those polynomial-whatevers. Who cares? And for that matter, I'm proud of my degree, and someday I'll get my PhD if I feel like it—or maybe not—but that has nothing to do with my mothering. I love Brady, he loves me, and we'll conquer this little hurdle in his life together."]

What am I fearing right now?

[I think I fear the intimidating way that teacher talked to me. I think I fear that my job is getting in the way of my responsibilities as a mother. I think I fear that I was just not assertive enough with Ms. Albright. I could have been more honest and open with her instead of immediately going into my "pathetic me" routine. Do I really think that Brady getting a low grade in a math class is going result in me losing something in my life? Lose my friends? Lose my husband, my kids? This is ridiculous thinking!]

Go!

[As you sit in the car in the school parking lot, after having prevented yourself from going into the funnel by using Confront and Scan, you think "Go. Okay. I have to do something now." So you start the car, turn on your favorite CD, and start belting out your favorite song. You avoided the funnel! Personal victory. Great training while you were right there in the trenches fighting the battle in your mind.]

TRAINING ON YOUR OWN

Now for a moment, look at these other thoughts, try CSG with them one-by-one, and see if you can make the process more automatic.

"Why didn't I read to him more when he was little?"

"*I never did* understand algebra. No wonder Brady is flunking."

"Why didn't my mom and dad help me more with math? Dad always did like Sarah more that he liked me."

"This is a joke. I'm a fraud as a parent. Why can't I do anything right?"

"Why hasn't Brady said anything about this? Am I *that* unapproachable as a parent?"

"Is there anything going right in my life? My kid is flunking out of school. What are the other parents going to think?"

"Poor Brady. He must be miserable carrying this around with him all the time. I haven't even asked him how his classes were going. Is it that I just don't care? Am I too tired to care? But how could I keep up with all that? Look at me: my hair is ugly, my kids are flunking out of school, and I'm twenty pounds overweight!"

Each one of these negative thoughts acts as a stimulus to your brain. By now you are seeing that you have that space of time between when you have the thought and when you respond. Always, always put your CSG thinking in that space. It must be automatic in your thinking, and the only way to make it automatic is by training.

If you feel overwhelmed at this point of the book and you don't have much self-confidence that you can actually change your ways, let us assure you that you're exactly where you should be. You are right on schedule!

WE DARE YOU

We dare you to go back through this chapter and actually memorize the CSG pattern with its simple questions. If you have it memorized, it will be there for you the next time your default setting shows up. Now, go train.

NOTE

1. David O. McKay, in Benson, "Think on Christ," *Ensign* (April 1984), 9.

seven

ONE HEAD—TWO VOICES

You've undoubtedly heard about the "left-brain/right-brain" models of the brain, the left side of the brain being the more logical side and the right brain being the more freethinking, creative side. That's all fine, but that isn't helping us get rid of the bad thoughts we think about ourselves when we make a mistake or when we compare ourselves to others.

We can do better in how we visualize how our brain is working, or we should say how our thinking works.

Let's imagine that you divide your brain in half: not left and right (so you don't confuse it with the above referenced model of the brain) but let's say the front half and the back half of the brain. Imagine that voices emanate from both halves: the back part of the brain is your Inner Critic and the front half is your Inner Voice.

These two distinct and separate voices speak to you all the time, depending on what your situation is. We have also seen this described as a little devil sitting on one shoulder and a little angel sitting on the other shoulder, both whispering things in your ears. We like the "voices in the head" visual better, because that's how so many women in our focus groups described it.

Let's dissect these two voices so we can learn what to do with them when they are talking to us.

THE INNER VOICE

Let's face it: we all talk to ourselves. We all have this chatter going on inside our heads—the internal commentary. The Inner Voice is more refined than the usual chatter, and it should be. Call it intuition, instinct, or perhaps conscience; this Inner Voice tells us that certain things are right and certain things are wrong. Animals seem to be driven by an instinct for survival. If a few of the weaker members of the herd are eliminated to help the rest of the group survive, animals don't seem to care.

Human beings, however, appear to be driven by something higher, something like a moral compass. We are driven by a sense of right and wrong. For example, every time I ride our local light rail train—especially when it is crowded—and an elderly person gets on, I instinctively stand and give up my seat. Nowhere on the train are there any posted signs indicating that I should do so. I do because deep in my soul I know that it's the right thing to do. And I usually find that I am not the only one with the instinct to stand.

The next time you drive, notice how many other drivers are generally obeying the traffic laws. Certainly there will be a few who do not, but the great majority will stop at red lights and stop signs, will signal when they change lanes, and will drive an appropriate speed. Our society works because the majority of people in it have an instinct to do what is right.

That inner urging to do the right things, to think the right things, to believe the right things is what we call your Inner Voice.

It can be delicate, restrained, even sensitive. But it gives you the direction you needed at that moment, because it's the truth within you.

Your Inner Voice seems to come from a different place than the normal running commentary or conversation you have with yourself. It has a much different quality and character.

Your Inner Voice is your friend. It is your "true coach." It will always tell you the truth and never lead you astray.

So the question would be: how can I hear or feel my Inner Voice more frequently? Great question. First, we have to start being aware that we even *have* an Inner Voice. Once we are aware that we do, we can start discovering more about it.

Tuning in to the Inner Voice requires listening with the heart. It's not audible. Listening takes time and quiet. Most of the women we have interviewed just laughed when we suggested they take a time-out during the day to just sit still, be quiet, and listen. But when some of them dared to take five minutes amid the hustle and bustle of the average day, it started making a difference. They coped better with the day. They were more apt to feel the pull of the heart telling them that they were okay. They said that it was so much easier for them to pick up on the Inner Critic and throw her out.

We didn't tell them to meditate. We didn't give them a prescribed way of doing anything. We just told them to sit quietly for five minutes and listen deep down inside themselves. When one woman asked, "So, what am I supposed to listen for?" we told her, "We have no idea. Listen for feelings of the heart. Listen for validation. Listen for confirmation. Each one of you will feel different things as you sit silently. Your mind will tend to wander off to all the things you have to still accomplish that day. Bring your mind back, over and over again, to listening quietly to your heart. Be still."

To reiterate, the ironic thing about that Inner Voice is that it is much more often *felt* than it is *heard*. Therein lies a key. It does not appear to be logical, but it is better in this case to "feel" an answer that to "think" an answer. If your mind is quieter, you can have a heightened awareness of those feelings. They are more "thoughts from the heart" than "thoughts from the mind."

Let us now introduce you to your enemy.

THE INNER CRITIC

This is the other voice. This is not a friendly voice. This is the "false coach." One author describes that voice this way:

> The Inner Critic is like the bit of a mirror that makes us see a distorted picture. It is that inner voice [Inner Critic] that criticizes us and speaks

about us in a disparaging way. It makes everything look ugly. Most of us are not even aware that it is a voice or a self speaking inside of us because its constant judgments have been with us since early childhood and its running critical commentary feels like a natural part of ourselves. It develops early in our lives, absorbing the judgments of the people around us and the expectations of the society in which we live.

No matter how much you try, you cannot please your Inner Critic. No matter how much you listen to it and try to change yourself in the way that it wants, it follows you and grows stronger. It is exactly like a parent who has been critical of you. Nothing that you do is okay.

"The answer is to learn how not to play the game.[1]

You can always recognize your Inner Critic. You will usually feel uncomfortable, strained, or slightly dark (no wonder—you are going into darkness and out of the light). However, your Inner Critic will rob you of your peace. As stated above, you can never be enough for your Inner Critic.

Even Wikipedia says,

The inner critic or "critical inner voice" is a concept used in popular psychology to refer to a subpersonality . . . that judges and demeans a person. . . . The inner critic is usually experienced as an inner voice attacking a person, saying that he or she is bad, wrong, inadequate, worthless, guilty, and so on. . . . The inner critic often produces feelings of shame, deficiency, low self-esteem, and depression. It may also cause self-doubt and undermine self-confidence. It is common for people to have a harsh inner critic that is debilitating.[2]

The problem is that the Inner Critic is a liar. It is the opposite of the Inner Voice. Your Inner Critic will deceive you. It will fool and trick you into believing what it's telling you. That's why you must train yourself to start listening to the Inner Voice—not the Inner Critic.

GIVE IT A NAME

Let's make the Inner Critic real. Some people call it a "gremlin." You can name it whatever you want, but for now let's just call it (her) Icy (for IC, or Inner Critic) We want you to learn to talk back to Icy whenever she is talking to you. Remember: Icy is *not* you. The real you comes from your Inner Voice.

Watch how talking to Icy can free you from her:

Karen's sister comes over for a short visit. As her sister comes through the front door, her first comment as she looks around is, "Hey, Sis, when did the bomb go off? This place is a mess!"

Karen laughs, but inside her head, Icy goes to work. What is the first thought that comes into Karen's head? "You've always been a lousy housekeeper. Your house is always a mess." Karen becomes aware that Icy is talking to her, so she talks back: "Oh, Icy, back again, huh? Thanks for your input. That's actually pretty funny. Big Sis has a housekeeper. Look, my house could be picked up better, but I'm doing the best I can here. I don't need you pickin' at me—so *get out of my head*! Stop spewing your crap on me!"

Icy will never go away. She'll keep coming back to try to get you. She was actually programmed in there from when you were a small child.

So which voice is more powerful, Icy or your Inner Voice? In the beginning Icy is much stronger because she is your habit. She is the product of uncontrolled thinking. As you learn to talk back to her, and then switch to your Inner Voice, the voice of truth, Icy will have much less effect on you.

It is essential to remember that Icy is a false voice, and your Inner Voice is more than a voice—it is a feeling, based on the truth, your moral compass, your instinct to be good and right. All throughout this book we stress the fact that the "truth will make you free." Chasing Icy away doesn't happen all at once; it takes practice. It's in the training. Practice talking back to Icy until it becomes automatic. When you find yourself beating up on yourself, stop and see what Icy is trying to get you to believe. She is the consummate liar. One woman told us that her beginning statement to Icy is always, "I see what you're trying to do to me. I'm on to ya!"

As discussed earlier, maybe you get some type of payoff or good feeling from letting Icy have a heyday in your brain. Does it feel good to let her run around in there? Or is it that you can switch on your "martyr syndrome" by letting Icy get to you. Those are both ways of avoiding responsibility. You can play the martyr, or pretend it feels gratifying to feel the pain of self-deprecation, but it's a cop-out. Sooner or later you will get tired of the whole self-deception and yearn for the truth. Your Inner Voice, that feeling from deep down inside you, will never lie. Listen to the real you. You are powerful. You are bigger than Icy. *You* control her. Of course it takes effort in the beginning, but the more you control Icy, the less power she has. Shine light on the darkness. Be aware of what you are thinking, then move into the light.

Two voices. One choice. Stop the internal drama by learning to talk back!

WE DARE YOU

We dare you to start verbally talking back to your inner critic today. Yes, out loud. Not so that all your coworkers can hear you ("That lady is nuts"). Just so you can hear it. Take personal responsibility for the voice you are listening to all day long.

We also dare you to take five minutes a day and just sit and listen. *Anyone* can take five minutes, can't they? And a hint, don't do it just before bedtime.

NOTES

1. Hal and Sidra Stone, *Embracing Your Inner Critic: Turning Self-Criticism into a Creative Asset*. (San Francisco: HarperSanFrancisco, 1993), 4–6.

2. "Inner critic," *Wikipedia*, September 17, 2013, accessed May 7, 2013, http://en.wikipedia.org/wiki/Inner_critic.

eight

THE SHIELD OF FAITH:
Identifying Your Triggers

EMOTIONAL TRIGGERS

Triggers are your friends. Triggers are your enemies. Every time you walk in a park and see a swing, your mind goes back to when your dad used to push you on the swing on sunny summer days. It was such a warm, loving feeling. Every time you bake bread, it takes you back to your grandmother's kitchen. Seeing her there with her hair pinned up, with the red-and-white checkered apron, baking her famous loaves. She always told you that someday you would grow up and bake bread for "your babies." You felt so accepted, so loved.

Those are positive triggers. Your emotional state immediately soars when these triggers do their thing. Those feelings can be quickly blown away when a negative emotional trigger appears on the scene.

You can think of some yourself, but let's look at a few: every time you see a yellow car it triggers the memory of your first boyfriend and the terrible experience you had with him in that truck. Or the old Beatles song that takes you back to junior high and the teacher that gave you a D on the report that you had put your heart and soul into. Or every time you see or smell good ol' apple crisp it triggers your mind back to when you vomited your apple crisp because you were so morning sick; now you can't stand the sight or smell of it—and it's been twenty-five years!

Another way of saying something "triggered my emotions" is saying something "really pushed by button." Let's look at some triggers that affect you, as a woman, in your day-to-day life, because once you get your button pushed, or your mind triggered, it's a slippery slope into the funnel of low self-worth from there.

Some common triggers that can take you quickly down the funnel if left unchecked:

- The dress that *used to* fit
- The bill collector
- The unfinished goals or dreams
- The new haircut
- The "other" mothers
- The fatigue
- The failed diet
- The mother-in-law
- The neighbor
- The email account with 1,756 unread e-mails
- The PMS
- The biggest one: The Mirror

Each one of the above triggers can elicit physical, emotional, mental and/or spiritual states. We cannot get away from them—they are all around us and have been since we were children. But the good thing about it is this: triggers are always based on some event from your past. It is not happening now, so you need to stay focused on the present.

Psychologists say that emotions are triggered because we think we are being threatened by someone or something. When your brain recognizes that someone is trying to take something away from you, it automatically triggers certain emotions. And what is it that you think might be taken away? Look at this list (there are plenty more):

- Acceptance

- Being loved
- Being treated fairly
- Being understood
- Being in control
- Peace
- Safety
- Predictability
- Autonomy
- Being right

Are any of these needs triggers for you if you think they might be taken away by someone? Let's try a couple on for size:

Remember the example of the D you got on your report in junior high school that you had worked so hard on? Now every time you hear a Beatles song it triggers an anger response toward not only that particular teacher, but also to most of your junior high years. As you look at this trigger, go back to the list above and see which things were being threatened by the poor grade. "Being treated fairly"? Maybe. Certainly "being understood" was threatened. And of course you were not in control, and your peace had been taken away, too. All those threats for all those years, and the Beatles songs still play on and on—only to keep triggering your emotions.

Psychologist Carl Jung wrote, "Everything that irritates us about others can lead us to an understanding of ourselves."

SO WHAT IF I GET TRIGGERED?

You might be asking, what's the big deal? So I have triggers. Everybody does. What does it have to do with Women's Weakness and how I feel about myself? Everything.

As stated, triggers can put you in an emotionally charged place many times each day. You go to church and see the perfect family sitting in front of you. Bam! The trigger goes off in your head about sitting with your family when you were a child. That was just before your parents separated and then divorced. That trigger is helping you lose peace in your life as you reflect on your supposed defects in your character because you came from a fractured family. Your acceptance has been threatened!

You pull into the gas station to fill up and bam! There's a woman with a trim little body wearing short shorts and a tank top at the next pump. It's the perfect trigger to take you back to your default setting of comparing your body to her body. Now your peace is threatened again, and you are not understood by others. (It doesn't even matter to you that she is divorced, broke, and hates herself—because you can't see that—all you see is her body.)

Your mother-in-law (or mother) comes over for dinner and makes a comment about the clutter in your home. Trigger! What is being threatened here? Your autonomy? Being in control? Acceptance? Not being understood? All of the above?

The point is each of these triggers can make you lose peace and happiness in your life, and when that is gone, you are standing at the low self-worth pitcher, waiting to take a huge drink of the Kool-Aid. You are falling for it hook, line, and sinker.

What we are asking you to do in this book is really what we call "emotional engineering." If you are going to change, if you are going to make progress in this life, you must engineer your emotions. You are triggered or *enticed* by someone or something to "lose your cool" and go into a self-esteem attack about thirty times a day.

Notice the word *enticed*. One dictionary definition of the word is to "be seduced" or to "be lured, bribed, or attracted to something."

We need to be the emotional engineers of ourselves—we must take control of our own emotions through controlling how we see and handle the triggers or enticements that come at us almost constantly.

As Pogo, the comic strip character philosophized, "We have met the enemy, and he is us."

Women cannot afford the luxury of allowing themselves to have these types of self-deprecating thoughts. They must be on the offensive. You cannot continue being your own worst enemy.

GIVING AWAY OUR FREEDOM TO CHOOSE

We all have the right to choose how we are going to react to different situations. Nobody can ever take our right to choose away from us. Or can they? You would be surprised to see how easily we let other people or other situations literally take away our freedom to choose.

We all fight so hard to be ourselves, to be totally independent from others, to not have to answer to anyone, and yet, as soon as we are triggered, we give our freedom or agency to someone else.

It is *imperative* that you understand what we mean here about "giving your agency or right to choose away to others."

Imagine yourself standing in a grocery checkout line. You are in somewhat of a hurry (the way we all tend to live our lives!). The man ahead of you in line is having a few problems: *three times* during his check out process price checks had to be called for. Your temper wears thin. When the checker asks, "Were you able to find everything you needed in our store today?" the answer is, "No—I couldn't find the ground flaxseed." That means another three-minute delay—which gets you to the breaking point. You feel yourself getting hotter (that's your sympathetic nervous system not being very sympathetic). You're thinking about how late you're going to be for a meeting. Your coworkers will chide you and your boss will give you *the look*. Now the flaxseed miraculously appears so he can finally get rung up—but wait—he has forgotten his checkbook and his credit card won't go through.

You get the picture. You finally get out to your car and call a coworker. "That guy was an idiot! He made me so mad!"

No. You allowed yourself to get mad. His behavior held you hostage. You got enticed—seduced! You got triggered, but it was *your* choice to let yourself get upset. His admittedly poor planning now had you enraged. It is as if you walked up to the man in front of you and said,

> "Here you go, sir. I'd like to give you my agency. I'd like you to control my emotions. Not even God will take away my right to choose, but I am giving it to you—of my own free will and choice. Yes, you really

got me this time. I was standing there in the checkout line and pretty much lost it emotionally because of your inconsiderate behavior. So here, take it. Hold out your hands, and I'll just dump my agency into yours. You're in control of me now. Wow, I can't believe I'm doing this, but you know, I do it all the time. As a matter of fact, just yesterday I gave three people my agency. I gave it to my sister when she called and said she wasn't going to be able to watch my kids this afternoon for my dental appointment. After I hung up, I just screamed—she made me so mad. And then right after that, the bank called and said our account was overdrawn. My husband didn't deposit his paycheck yesterday and I wrote four checks that will bounce. He makes me so upset when he forgets things like that. And to top it all off, our washing machine won't work and I've got at least six loads to do today! Argggh! That stupid machine gets me livid. So here, take my agency and shove it!"

Notice how you gave your agency away first to the man in the checkout line; second to your husband; and third to an inanimate object: the washing machine! It's a good thing the family dog wasn't nearby. It would have controlled her too! It is as if you had no choice in the matter anymore. You *had* to lose it, because that's what you do. You are out of control because you don't know how to handle a trigger when it comes at you. How many times a day do we give our agency away? Multiple times, and until we can recognize what is really going on inside our heads, it will continue.

This, in a way, becomes a game we play within ourselves. We call it "The Blame Game." Psychologists call it "disowning." The spiritual definition of disowning would read like this: "making someone else responsible for what is going on inside me." Disowning is a powerful tool that allows us to not have to take personal responsibility for anything in our lives. It's always someone else's fault.

The critical question is this: is there some kind of *payoff* for giving our agency to someone else—for blaming someone else for our unhappiness? Absolutely YES! The payoff is this: If we can blame someone else, then we don't have to *do* anything. We are not answerable for anything—no responsibility.

Let's look at a real-life example and see if you can identify with it.

I received a call from a distraught single mother, saying her teenage daughter was being held at the nearby grocery store for shoplifting. The police had told her that she needed to come down to the store and deal with the whole issue.

When she called me, she was upset, hurt, and embarrassed. I asked her why she felt those things. She said it was because of what her daughter had done. Because of her daughter's actions, she was humiliated and even angry.

Do you see the lie here? Yes, of course what the daughter did was wrong, and of course there will need to be consequences for her. But right now, in the thick of things, the mother is blaming her daughter for what she herself is feeling. She is disowning. We all do it. Why is disowning so popular? Because the disowner then doesn't have to change—the other person (in the disowner's eyes) is the one that needs to change.

Do you see here how she has given her agency away to the situation? She has given it to her daughter and the police, because she had allowed herself to become angry, embarrassed, resentful, and hurt that her daughter would ever do such a thing. She is no longer in control of her emotions. She has let the situation trigger her. Now she feels like a failure as a mother. "What if the women in the neighborhood hear about this? I thought we taught her better than this. What about all the family discussions on honesty?"

And when really confronted with the truth of the situation that she has given the power of her agency away to her daughter and the police, she responds, "What do you mean my anger and disappointment doesn't come from my daughter's behavior? Are you crazy? I don't deserve this to happen to me. I am so upset."

Yes, she was upset, and she let the whole scenario control her, thus giving her agency away. Can you imagine how she will treat her daughter when she gets her alone in the car on the way home from dealing with the police? Having given her agency away to the entire situation, she will probably forget that it's not about the situation at all: it's all about the relationship she has with her daughter.

Let us now examine a valuable tool in combating the propensity to disown, to blame, to give our agency away, because these behaviors always weaken our resolve to do away with Women's Weakness.

THE SHIELD

There is a solution. You can overcome these tendencies. The tool you can use we call "The Shield."

Many years ago I, Robert, lived in Germany. I had the opportunity one day to visit an authentic castle built in the Dark Ages, which was preserved quite nicely. I walked through all of the rooms, but the one that really caught my attention was called the armor room. This was the room that was lined on both sides with the armor suits you see in movies, all made out of metal. Some were shiny and smooth. Some were not. These were the knights' armor. Each had a shield held by either arm. As I progressed to the far end of the long hall, passing by all the "knights in shining armor" I came to the end, where the king's armor was displayed. The interesting thing was his shield: it was all banged up. One could readily see that he had fought in some pretty good battles. Lots of dings and dents. It served him well over many years. The sign said he ended up dying from the Black Death, not in battle. His shield protected him through thick and thin.

Let's face it. Every day we get lots of dings and dents in our protective shields. We can call them triggers, enticements, buttons that someone pushes, or swords and arrows. We can't avoid them, but the rather amusing thing about our human nature is we sometimes go about our days as if they are non-existent! We strike out on our daily journey thinking all is well, expecting the very best to happen all day long, not suspecting that right around the corner there is a sword or axe heading towards us. A situation. A disappointment. A person. A delay. So we get triggered. We get enticed. Somebody or something pushes our button and we end up giving our agency away again and again.

The Shield, then, is the effective, protective mental tool we use to fend off all the triggers that happen to us everyday, long *before* the trigger attacks us. It's what prevents us mentally from getting hooked by the offending person or situation.

Author Stephen Covey included the following quote, which seems appropriate to our discussion, in one of his books: "Between stimulus and response there is a space. In that space lies our freedom and power to choose our response. In those choices lie our growth and our happiness."[1]

We like to paraphrase that statement like this: Between stimulus and response is a space (or gap). What we do with that space will determine how much happiness, peace, contentment, and joy we will have in our lives.

When we are triggered there is a space of time. That space may be a millisecond, or it may be days or weeks. How we respond to those triggers or enticements or adversities, day after day, week after week, lays a foundation of our characters, which eventually reaps our destiny.

When we get triggered, we get hooked. Our expectations about situations get us hooked emotionally. Example:

In a family discussion with your husband and children, you discuss with your children the fact that, as the mom, it is not your responsibility to make your children's beds every morning. You all have a good dialogue about it and the conclusion reached is that all the children (the one's that are physically capable) will make their beds before they go to school every morning. It's a done deal. You feel relieved that the decision has been made.

The next morning you hear the last "Bye, Mom" as the front door shuts. You go upstairs to scout out the bedrooms.

Ask yourself this question before opening the first door: what are your expectations?

If you enter any of the rooms expecting the beds to be made, you set yourself up. You didn't have your "Shield" up in front of you. The first unmade bed has you hooked, and you get frustrated. The second unmade bed makes you sad; the third makes you angry. By the fourth unmade bed, you mumble something about "Oh, what's the use!" And then you mumble something about "Wait till those kids get home!" and "I'm such a lousy mother!"

Had the Shield been up, you would not have had to give your agency away to your children. A shield is there to protect you from harm. You would remember it's not about beds, but relationships. And expectations. Can you imagine that German king going into battle without his shield? Your Shield prevents those triggers from getting to you and striking a fatal blow. Here's how:

Change your expectations. Yes, it's that simple. If you go into the bedrooms really expecting that after *one* family discussion your children will remember what they agreed to (which requires them to immediately change their bad habits) your expectations need to be labeled as "unrealistic."

- *Old Expectation:* all four of my children will make their beds perfectly every day for the rest of their lives.
- *New Expectation:* none of my children will remember to make their beds tomorrow morning; this is a work in progress and will take time and patience.

Again, it's our expectations regarding these recurring events in our lives that get us hooked all day long. This is *not* to say that we shouldn't have great expectations throughout our lives. But when it comes to others' disappointing behaviors, whether it be our children, our spouse, our friends or relatives, we cannot afford to continually allow their behavior to rule us and "make us so mad."

What if, in the above bed-making scenario, the mother would have had a little self-talk before she went upstairs and said something like this:

"Okay, Susan, before you go into the kids' bedrooms, remember that they are still children: don't expect that any of the beds are made, and that's okay. If even one bed is made, that's okay, but I refuse to get hooked today. I will not give my agency away. I love these kids."

Would a quick chat like that have refocused you? Of course it would have; but the main thing is that technique is one of the most effective ways of putting up the Shield. Remember:

Stimulus → Space of Time → Response

We find that, when the stimulus hits, it helps very much to slow the whole process down. We can do that by concentrating on the space of time just before you start to be self-critical. The objective is to make a mental space for your thinking so you have time to analyze or dissect what is going on in your head *before* you jump into the funnel of low self-worth, not after. Once you jump into the funnel, it's a hundred times harder to get out than it is to just back away from the funnel before ever going in. So the key is:

FOCUS ON THE GAP

Another way of putting this would be that as soon as we are aware of the stimulus (a.k.a. getting triggered) we *freeze* our thoughts until we can detach ourselves from them. We take a step back and look at what's going on right then.

Let's look at another personal example regarding Women's Weakness with two possible outcomes.

The Cooking Class

You've been waiting almost two years for your husband to say yes to the gourmet natural foods cooking class offered by the local grocery store. You can't believe the time has come when he actually consented to go with you. Something always came up, but after dropping enough hints, he said he'd go, and now he is even looking forward to being with you there and learning together.

The night of the first of four classes comes. You dress in a cute outfit and coach him on not wearing the jeans he used to do yard work in, so he wore his nice slacks and sports shirt. This was going to be a great evening. Even your hair turned out perfectly, which it so seldom does. You drive to the store and find the place for the class and walk in. There are five or six other couples milling around talking, and everyone seems excited to be there.

The instructor begins the class by having every couple introduce themselves and tell why they came to the class. One of the couples is obviously a little pretentious and even flashy—the kind that you find quite annoying because they try so hard to impress everyone else in the group. The problem is it didn't stop with the introductions. It went on the whole evening. At one point the wife even flirted with one of the other husbands.

The class itself was filled with great information, but the one flashy couple was so distracting that it kind of bugged you throughout the whole evening. Your husband just laughed about it and shrugged it off. You didn't.

On the drive home you brought it up—how irritated you were with the couple and that you hoped they wouldn't come back next week.

Scenario #1

Next week came, and sure enough, they were there again, in "all their glory" as you described it to your husband as soon as you saw them. That morning as you got dressed you again mentioned to your husband that you hoped that couple didn't come back. During the day you felt yourself getting a little more uptight as the day went on, even to the point that you didn't even know if you wanted to go to the class that night if "they" were there.

As you walked into the classroom, you saw her. She was in a tight-fitting red dress. *A dress? Who wears a dress to a cooking class?* you thought to yourself. She was loud, almost over-the-top, as she laughed and looked around to see who was watching. When the instructor entered the room, she gushed over him. You thought to yourself again, *She is so irritating. Who does she think she is? I can't stand women like that.*

You watched her the whole night. You barely heard what the instructor said. For you, the class had been ruined, and you told your husband on the way home that you didn't want to go back. He mumbled something about that he thought the food samples were great and there were some guys there that were pretty nice. Your reaction? "My husband is clueless."

Scenario #2

Next week came, but you had contemplated the situation during the week and you knew that "that woman" had really gotten to you. Since you knew it bothered you last week, you also knew that you were very vulnerable to letting her "psych you out" again tonight if you didn't first put up your Shield. Her personality was a major trigger for you, but you knew how to deal with triggers.

As you were coming back from dropping off your kids to school that morning, you decided to stay focused by having a little chat with yourself:

Okay, Laurie, you know how that woman at the cooking class bothered you last week. You don't want to react that way, but you're really gonna need help when you get to class tonight. But I'm not gonna set myself up. I fully expect to see her flirt and be loud and try to attract all the attention to her again tonight, so I'm going to see the situation for what it is. I refuse to feel diminished by her. I will not give her my agency! I'm going to love her with my thoughts, even when she ignores me, which I know she will. I expect her to behave maybe even worse tonight than she did last night, but it's okay. I'm not going to get triggered at all.

That night you and your husband walk across the parking lot of the grocery store. You do a little more self-talk again (part of putting the Shield up) that you won't get triggered. You walk into the classroom and there she is, but this time you see her differently. You see her as a struggling woman, who is probably just as insecure as you are but who covers it up by her outward behavior. As she works so hard to attract all the attention, you inwardly smile, knowing that, at least for tonight, you're okay—you're not triggered, nor hooked by her behavior or anybody else's. Your Shield is up—the fiery darts cannot pierce you tonight. You decide that that time between stimulus and response is, indeed, one of the best ways to keep the Shield up *every day*.

Which scenario do you choose?

The great thing about this technique is this: you can and should use it multiple times per day. Here is another scenario, one that we've seen before:

You're driving down the street on a beautiful, sunny day. Everything is going your way. You feel proud of yourself because you are even driving two miles per hour below the speed limit! Then, all of a sudden, a car pulls out from a side street and gets in front of you! You have to slow down to a crawl. You lose it! You throw your arms in the air and scream out loud in the car, "What are you thinking?" The car continues to proceed at a snail's pace, and you continue your rant. "Oh, for cryin' out loud—you've go to be kidding me! Really? Get off the road, lady. You should get your license taken away."

Finally there's a chance to pass, so you gun your car and speed by, making sure to *glare* at the driver. That driver didn't even look at you as you sped by. She looked as if she were maybe in her late seventies, silver hair, glasses, hands firmly positioned at ten and two o'clock. But you didn't care, because you had long since relinquished your freedom and agency to her. No siree, no stimulus and response. She had you hooked, and the most hilarious thing about it is she has no idea that she hooked you. She is still having a wonderful sunny day. You aren't.

Let us ask you something very important: as you left your garage that morning, what did you expect? Did you expect perfect drivers (like yourself) to fill the streets, and that nobody makes mistakes? Could we say that might be an unrealistic expectation, just like expecting your children to make all their beds the first time you ask them?

Scenario Reset

As you back out of your garage that morning, you remind yourself that there will probably be at least ten discourteous drivers on the road that morning, and that you will use them as a test to see if you can keep from getting hooked. Besides, you have made it a game to see how many stimulus/response episodes you can notice in one day. You are setting yourself up in a great way by putting up that Shield before the fiery darts come at you.

You're driving down the street on a beautiful, sunny day. Everything is going your way. You feel proud of yourself because you are even driving two miles per hour below the speed limit! Then all of a sudden from a side street on your right out pulls a car in front of you! You have to slow down to a crawl. (**Stimulus**!)

(**Response**) You start laughing out loud and say to yourself, "That's amazing. I'm not even four blocks from home, and I got my first one today. Aha, it looks like a little old lady up there in that car. I'll bet she's driving to the rest home to visit her husband who has Alzheimer's. Bless her heart!"

Which story was the better one? That's totally up to you—but if you are looking to overcome your natural tendencies to lose it whenever something doesn't go exactly your way (human nature for all men and women), you probably want to choose the Scenario Reset. It provides you with much more happiness in life. It makes life easier, believe us.

> My father taught me to always be more tolerant of people who sin differently than I do. (Author unknown)

How much time was there between the Stimulus and the Response? One second maybe? Sometimes you will have to choose your response, but it will affect you sometimes for years to come. The key is to set yourself up before, so it doesn't always catch you off guard so easily.

A classic quotation from C. S. Lewis in *Mere Christianity* describes what suddenness can do to us and shows us who we really are inside:

> We begin to notice, besides our particular sinful acts, our sinfulness; begin to be alarmed not only about what we do, but about what we are. This may sound rather difficult, so I will try to make it clear from my own case. When I come to my evening prayers and try to reckon up the sins of the day, nine times out of ten the most obvious one is some sin against charity; I have sulked or snapped or sneered or snubbed or stormed. And the excuse that immediately springs to my mind is that the provocation was so sudden and unexpected; I was caught off my guard, I had not time to collect myself. Now that may be an extenuating circumstance as regards those particular acts:

they would obviously be worse if they had been deliberate and pre-meditated. On the other hand, surely what a man does when he is taken off his guard is the best evidence for what sort of a man he is? Surely what pops out before the man has time to put on a disguise is the truth? If there are rats in a cellar you are most likely to see them if you go in very suddenly. But the suddenness does not create the rats: it only prevents them from hiding. In the same way the suddenness of the provocation does not make me an ill-tempered man; it only shows me what an ill-tempered man I am. The rats are always there in the cellar, but if you go in shouting and noisily they will have taken cover before you switch on the light.[2]

Notice that Lewis says, "I had not time to collect myself." In our hurried lives, we must "collect" ourselves, otherwise the world will hook us every time. Frankly, there are hundreds of stimuli everyday, waiting to hook us. But guess what? *Life is designed that way on purpose!* It's supposed to be that way for our growth. We receive trials in our lives (stimuli) to give us tiny little growth experiences each day. It's how we respond to each one that provides us with happiness and contentment, or misery.

When we realize that our spouse, our children, our parents, our neighbors, our friends, are all placed around us as stimuli, then we start to get the true picture of life. "You mean, my husband could be my greatest opportunity for growth?" Yes. And you are *his* greatest opportunity for growth too. "The suddenness of the provocation" that Lewis talks about can indeed be your spouse or an in-law, showing you what an ill-tempered person you might be . . . if you don't use that space of time between stimulus and response . . . every time a trigger comes.

So let's go back to that original list of potential triggers:

- The dress that *used* to fit
- The bill collector
- The unfinished goals or dreams
- The new haircut
- The "other" mothers
- The fatigue

- The failed diet
- The mother-in-law
- The neighbor
- The email account with 1,756 unread emails
- The PMS
- The biggest one: The Mirror

Can you now see how each one of these is a stimulus? Can you see that you have a space of time before you respond? Can you see how easy it is to literally "give your agency away" in each case? Let's look at a few:

The new haircut: a common trigger for women. What is the unrealistic expectation? That your stylist will do a *perfect* cut and color. (Ha!) You set yourself up for that one, didn't you?

The fatigue: a constant trigger in your life. The expectation? "Today I will have the energy I need to make it a good day." You set yourself up by not going to bed the night before until midnight. The fatigue happens. Triggered.

Your mother-in-law is coming for dinner. The expectation? She won't say anything that irritates you. That's like saying you can drive from California to Florida and never have anyone do something stupid in traffic right in front of you. Again, an unrealistic expectation! (We ask all mothers-in-law for forgiveness for this example.)

In each of these three examples, we challenge you to find the better response—the response that will make you the happier person, not the upset, angry, distressed person you could have chosen to be.

Using the stimulus-space-response model is a powerful tool you can use multiple times per day to keep you out of the low self-esteem funnel.

WE DARE YOU

We dare you to start each day with the expectation of multiple triggers throughout your day. Stop setting yourself up to be triggered. Look forward to the triggers and start talking to yourself when they appear. See them for what they really are: opportunities to grow, to gain greater self-mastery. Whenever you leave your home, or answer the telephone, just expect some type of a trigger, and put up your Shield! Create that new habit.

NOTES

1.   Stephen Covey, *The 7 Habits of Highly Effective Families* (New York: Golden Books, 1998), 27.

2.   C. S. Lewis, *Mere Christianity* (New York: HarperCollins, 1952), 192.

nine

SEEING IS BELIEVING; BELIEVING IS SEEING

Philosophers, mystics, and prophets have described the next "tool" we will give you to help you overcome Women's Weakness or the propensity for many women to talk negatively about themselves to themselves. It's called "the mind's eye." It is the ability of the mind to envision or picture things, events, or memories.

The mind is like a video camera, recording everything through its senses: sight, sound, smell, touch, and taste. Although we cannot record some of the senses visually, we nevertheless record them in the brain—or the mind's eye.

I remember reading *The Hobbit* by J. R. R. Tolkien back in 1976. When I think of the book now, I still see scenes of the book that I created in my mind almost forty years ago! The mind is so powerful, and if we can use it to overcome our negative views of ourselves, we win the war.

Think of the last time you had a good old-fashioned nightmare. Was it real? No. Did it seem real? Absolutely. Your heart was probably pounding as you woke up. You wanted to get the dream out of your mind as quickly as possible. It wasn't real, but your body interpreted it as such. Its physical effect on you was real.

Look at the word *imagery*. It is defined as the formation of mental images, figures, or likenesses of things. This ability that we all have will be our tool. However, one person can view an event or read a statement and interpret it one way, while another person can view exactly the same thing and have a totally different viewpoint. It is true that "we see what we want to see." We are going to now use imagery, or the ability to form pictures in our minds.

This tool has three simple parts:

Imagine it—Image it—Experience it

We all do this all the time without really thinking about it. Now we will do it *under controlled thinking circumstances*. We will create it inside our minds. This tool is tremendously subconsciously powerful if practiced. Here's how it works:

Imagine it: this part is simple. You will pull up in your mind a situation that you have either already experienced or that you think you might experience wherein you have someone do something to you that you see as a put-down, a dig, or some other type of behavior that you interpret as devaluing to you.

Think briefly about what happened, who was there, and how you felt about the interaction. Most likely, during or after the little interaction, you thought something about yourself, or even whispered something about yourself to yourself. Did you feel rejected? What was your reaction? Did you get embarrassed? Did you immediately emotionally withdraw from the situation? Did you sabotage yourself? What was the final result of the interaction? Again, how did you *feel?* Did you "go chemical"? Did you go into the "funnel"?

We are going to give you several examples of this, but right now it's important for you to think of sometime in your past where this has happened to you (it should not take too much to think of an experience!).

Image it: This takes a quiet place with no distractions. This is part of your training, which can be done in just minutes per day.

When you have a quiet moment, maybe just before bed, or maybe even while driving, you are going to bring up that situation that you imagined above. You will now picture it all in your mind's eye, seeing every detail slowly as the experience unfolded.

Experience it: As you start to feel the rejection, as you see the look on that person's face as she made the unkind remark, as you feel yourself "going chemical" and ready to jump into the funnel of self-deprecation, you will now picture yourself literally using CSG in your mind. You see yourself going through the steps of Confront-Scan-Go. You use the mind's ability to create this mental picture or imagine while you are just sitting there.

This is called having a *private victory* (in your mind) before your *public victory* (the next time one of these situations happens to you for real). The private victory is crucial to your overcoming Women's Weakness. You must practice this in your mind, so that when the situation arises, your response is automatic—because it has been played out in your mind *before* it ever happened.

We hear of basketball players visualizing themselves standing at the foul line shooting free throws at a crucial time in a game. They practice this in their minds over and over, seeing in their mind's eye the ball swishing through the net. They see it, they hear it, they feel it. Research shows that this practicing in their minds can be *more effective* than actually physically standing in the gym and shooting the ball.

We want you to practice your worst-case scenarios over and over in your mind. Doing this shifts you from powerlessness to powerfulness. Remember what Eleanor Roosevelt said, "No one can make you feel inferior without your consent."

In a way, if you don't use this tool and train your thinking, you are giving consent to others to make you feel inferior. Having a private victory in your head is worth all the effort, because the more you practice with this tool, the more automatic it becomes.

In the following scenarios, watch to see what happens. Remember, these are not real, these are imagined, engineered-in-the-mind scenarios that are anticipated to happen in the future. Imagine it—Image it—Experience it.

1. KATIE

Katie's father-in-law, Rex, knows exactly how to push her buttons—not that he means to. He's a great guy, but sometimes he makes little remarks that make her think she is not good enough for his son. So next Sunday her in-laws are coming for dinner. Saturday night Katie decides to "put on her armor" by sitting down in her bedroom by herself. She actually pictures herself standing in her kitchen cooking the meal. She sees her father-in-law come through the front door and immediately come into the kitchen. In her imaging, she feels what is happening when he comes over to the stove and says, "Lasagna? We just had that last night! *Nobody* makes a better lasagna than my wife!"

In her mind, Katie sees the funnel. She feels herself going from thought to chemical, but she is practicing right now, and the idea of practicing this *before* it happens in real time is for her to automatically go to CSG.

As her father-in-law strolls out of the kitchen, Katie spontaneously confronts her situation by saying in mind, "Well, I knew it would happen. I'm not to give my power over to him. I see what's happening here. He's implying that I'm not as good a cook as his wife. I'm *not* gonna jump in the funnel (**Confront**).

Now she does her quick self-scan (**Scan**): *"Is it true?* Am I a lousy cook? No. I may not make the world's best lasagna, but I *am* a good cook; my husband loves my cooking and so do the kids."

"What am I fearing right now? Rex? Ha! He's a teddy bear. Am I fearing he thinks I'm not good enough for his son, that his son made a mistake? Yeah, that's probably the fear in the back of my mind. But after these eleven years of marriage, I know that's not true either. Rex loves me, even though sometimes he's kind of thoughtless."

[Stop! Do you realize that this is not real time? This is just a practice run for when the real thing happens tomorrow at dinner. Katie is only *imagining* this right now.]

"Am I going into darkness or light? Wow! Normally I would have let Rex really get to me. I'd be ticked off at him and maybe would have said some sarcastic remark back to him (probably under my breath). I can actually feel myself staying in the light. I feel freer than I normally would. This is cool!"

Now Katie practices **Go!** She has to do something right now. She hears herself saying to Rex, "Hey Rex, I didn't get my hug when you came in. Get over here!"

Katie gets up from her chair in the bedroom. She smiles. She says out loud, "Okay, Rex, bring it on!" She was ready for Sunday dinner to happen. She was "loaded for bear" as they say. She would be looking forward to Rex and his button-pushing ways, because that allows her to practice CSG. As a matter of fact, she'll be disappointed if Rex *doesn't* give her the opportunity!

2. EMMA

Emma is eighteen years old and is a freshman away at college. She has struggled with low self-worth most of her life, but she is making a huge effort, with her mother, to make positive adjustments to her feelings about herself. Now that she was living in a dorm with many other girls her age, she was worried about fitting in. She was great student, but, in her opinion, she was lacking in the social area. So one night, while she was alone in her room, she decided to try a short session of Imagine it-Image it-Experience it.

As she sat in her room she pictured herself walking down the hall in her dorm, seeing a bunch of the "popular girls" gathered together in one of the rooms. She saw herself walking slowly past the door of the noisy room and having a few of the girls look up at her, and then they immediately turned back to what they were doing, basically not acknowledging her at all.

(Confront) Even though this is a practice session, even though this is all in her mind, she could feel her heart beating a little faster due to the anxiety this picture was creating in her. "Yep, I've been there many times—the outsider. I can see where this is leading. I'm not going to let it happen right now. I've felt this rejection before. I'm getting that "pathetic me" thinking right now."

(Scan) Is it true that I'm pathetic, just because I'm not in there with them? Is there a lie in there somewhere? My old way says I'm pathetic, but my new way says, "Grow up, Emma. These girls don't know you at all. That's why I'm here in the hall. It's almost as if I'm pushing *my own buttons*. They don't mean any harm. They're probably all just as insecure as I am."

"What am I fearing right now? Uh, let's see. Obviously rejection. Not fitting in? Okay, that's typical. What else? Probably that I could live a lonely freshman year if I'm not in this 'in group. Oh, man, this is *really* pathetic. These are all made-up fears!"

"Let's see . . . light or dark? This is crazy! I'm heading into darkness just sitting here in my dorm room. I want to be in the light. It feels so much better there."

"**Go!** Okay, what can I do here right now in my mind?" She pictures herself running back down the hall to her room, grabbing the bag of homemade chocolate chip cookies her Mom had sent her. She then runs back to the room with the girls, walks in the room and announces, "Treat time! I'm Emma, and I've got cookies!" She sees the girls scrambling for the sack of cookies with shouts of glee!

Again, this was a dry run. She just had her private victory, which must always precede her *future* public victory.

3. NIKKI

Nikki got a new gym membership but was really afraid to use it. After the birth of her second child, she had gained a lot of weight and could never seem to lose it. She was embarrassed to be seen at the gym in work out clothes. Having heard about CSG from a friend, she decided to sit down and go through her first visit to the gym in her mind the night before right there in her kitchen. She sees herself sitting outside of the gym in the parking lot, fighting with herself about who she is and how she looks. It takes her ten minutes to just get up the courage to go in. She pictures herself walking through the front door of the gym and checking in at the front desk. She walks around the corner and sees all the people and the cardio machines.

(Confront) She found herself wanting to avoid the bad thoughts she was having about herself. She began trying to ignore her thoughts. Wrong! These thoughts must be confronted as they happen. She said to herself, "Whoa! What's happening here? Do I always do this to myself? I'm feeling like everyone is staring at me. For crying out loud! This is actually hilarious to see what I'm doing to myself!"

So far, so good! She stood up to herself, didn't run away from her self-critical thoughts, and stared them right in the face!

(Scan) "Am I a loser for just wanting to get in shape? No. Is everyone staring at me? Ha! Don't flatter yourself, Nikki Thompson. Am I overweight? Yes, but that has nothing to do with who I *am*. I'm through telling myself all the lies."

"Now, what am I fearing? That these people are going to reject me? I don't even *know any of them here*! How can they reject me? Am I fearing I'm going to fall off the treadmill? That I'll work out, spend all this time and effort, and not lose a pound? Well, that could happen. But at least I'm here! I know it's healthy whatever else happens."

"Um, oh yeah, light and darkness. Geez, I was starting to go into darkness sitting in the car out there. Now that I'm analyzing my thinking, this is ridiculous! Darkness feels lousy. I didn't sign up for this gym membership to feel lousy. I choose to stay in the light."

Sitting in her kitchen, she smiles as she is going through this mental preparation. Just like the basketball player shooting his mental foul shots, she is picturing herself going to the gym and having this experience, and it hasn't even happened yet.

(Go!) She pictures herself getting off the treadmill, walking over to the drinking fountain. She imagines another woman standing there getting a drink. As that woman turns around, Nikki says, "That is the cutest workout outfit. Where did you get it?" Then ensues an imaginary fun conversation, which turns into a new friend at the gym.

And Nikki hadn't even left here home yet! That's tomorrow morning, but she has already worked through the trauma of the "first day back at the gym" thing, so she's going to be just fine.

In all three of the above examples, each of those women practiced *Stimulus—Response* in their minds eye before it happened in real life. That is their armor, their Shield.

We hope you see now that if you choose NOT to do these mental preparation sessions, you are setting yourself up . . . for getting hooked by anything or anyone that comes your way, because the world is set up to actually help us practice. Katie has her father-in-law. Emma has the girls in the dorm. Nikki has the people at the gym. It's all by design to help us grow out of this. We get smacked in the face daily by those who are inconsiderate, impolite, rude, uncaring, or mean. Those people are put right in our path *to help our growth*. We should be excited every time someone pushes us toward our funnel. They're just trying to help!

In these examples, as stated above, we are, in a way, pushing our own buttons. Those people were innocent bystanders. In other circumstances it can be a person that antagonizes or triggers us. Whichever it is, we have that space of time to decide which way we will go with our thoughts *before* we react.

Sometimes the people we love *the most* are our greatest reasons for our growth, because they know exactly what buttons to push. If we let all our "button-pushers" control us, throw us right into our funnel, we are powerless. But now you have tools.

Use your ability to imagine, image, and experience. It will save you time, anxiety, and tears.

WE DARE YOU

As part of your training, we dare you to start the day by picking one of your favorite triggers and working through it mentally. See the trigger coming at you, see yourself doing CSG. See the outcome (your private victory) before it ever happens. This creates so much power, it will surprise you every time you use it!

ten

CHANGE YOUR THOUGHTS

We saw in the first part of this book that both Men's Weakness and Women's Weakness start with a thought. Learning to control those thoughts is one of the most important skills of our lives. So much of who and what we are can be traced back to what we think. "As a man thinketh in his heart, so is he" (Proverbs 23:7). Choosing which thoughts are granted permission to stay and which are expelled, will not only define who you are, but it will also determine what you think about yourself.

Removing a thought from your head is a simple skill in theory. In practice, it can be a bit more challenging, because you have just a brief moment in which to succeed. If a thought is allowed to linger in your mind, it makes itself at home and becomes a much more difficult renter to evict. That is when it starts to trigger all sorts of emotions within you, and you are on to a more difficult challenge.

The key to this skill is understanding one simple truth about your amazing brain, which can only think of one thing at a time. Granted, it can move very quickly from one thought to another and back again, but it can only think of one thing at a time, like a stage that can only have one scene showing at any given moment.

Therefore, by choosing what *is* on the stage of your mind, you are also choosing what is *not* on stage. Undesirable thoughts can be removed simply by choosing to think of something else.

Try it. Think of a beautiful sunset, on a beach. That's a very pleasant image. Now think of a mountain scene with trees and a stream. Notice that the instant you thought of the mountain, the sunset disappeared. That's it. That's the skill. You just removed one thought by thinking of something else.

However, odds are that you are now discovering the challenge of controlling your thoughts. Yes, you got the sunset to disappear by thinking about the mountain. How long was it gone? Did the sunset disappear for good? If you are like most people, after a brief moment, the sunset was back and the mountain disappeared.

The real challenge, then, is not to *remove* a thought from your mind, but to *keep* that thought from returning. Yes, your mind can think of only one thing at a time, but it can quickly switch back. This requires a bit more concentration.

Try it again. Think of the sunset. Make it a pleasant picture that you enjoy having in your mind. Now think of the mountain scene. In a moment the sunset will try to come back onto the stage. When it does, focus your attention on the mountain. Keep it in your mind. Enjoy the mountain, the trees, the cool stream. Every time the sunset tries to come back into your mind, focus your attention on the mountain. Eventually the sunset will stop trying to reappear and you will have won the battle. Until that moment arrives, it will take concentrated effort to keep the sunset out of your thoughts.

This is the real challenge with regards to controlling your thoughts. You must first remove the negative thought from your mind and then you must keep it out. Having a "go-to" thought on which you can focus your attention will help keep that negative thought out.

Music is a powerful "go-to" thought. Many people will sing a favorite song until a thought leaves for good. Others will recite a favorite quotation or concentrate on a favorite memory.

WE DARE YOU

Your assignment is to find a "go-to" thought; something that you will use to replace and keep the negative thoughts about yourself away. The next time a thought pops into your head that suggests in any way that you are not good enough, pull out your "go-to" thought and get that negative thought off your stage. When it tries to return, keep your focus on your "go-to" thought. You may have to pull it out a thousand times, but if it keeps those destructive thoughts away, it is worth it.

eleven

CHANGE YOUR EMOTIONS

Many of this book's tools will help you change and control the negative thoughts you have about yourself. However, what do you do if you let the thoughts linger and they become emotions. Is there any way to change your emotions? Can you pull yourself out of the funnel?

The answer is, "Yes!" It is more difficult to change your emotions than to change your thoughts, but it can be done. You do not need to get pulled into nor stay in the funnel. You can change your emotions. If you don't, your emotions will change you.

The secret is to understand that emotions come from the stories that we tell ourselves. We start with facts; things we see and hear. We then interpret those facts; we tell ourselves a story. That story creates an emotion. We then act on that emotion. The facts do not create your emotions, your interpretation of those facts—your story—creates your emotions. If you want to change your emotion, you have to change your story. Here is an example:

You are driving down an old country road when you notice a teenager ahead in the distance, standing on the side of the road. As you approach, he reaches down, picks up a rock, and cocks his arm. "He wouldn't dare . . . ," you tell yourself. As you get within range, he throws the rock at your windshield, cracking it.

At that moment, you tell yourself a story about that young man. You probably tell yourself that he is a horrible punk kid with no respect for other people's property. After all, you clearly saw him pick up a rock and throw it at your car. That story instantly creates an emotion: Anger! With your blood boiling, you now act on that anger. You slam on your brakes. You are going to grab that boy, yell and scream at him, and then call the police. However, as soon as you stop, everything changes.

The young man runs up to your car and says, "Oh, thank you, ma'am, for stopping. I'm sorry about your window. I didn't know how else to stop you. My brother is in the ditch bleeding very badly. He's going to die if we don't get him some help. Please help us!" You look closely at his hands and they are covered in blood. Instantly, your emotion changes. Your anger has changed to compassion.

So, what happened? Your windshield is still cracked. The teenager still threw a rock at it. Those facts have not changed. Why are you now feeling compassion instead of anger? The answer is that your story changed. This young man went from being a scoundrel to a desperate brother trying to save a life. The truth is that you probably would not have stopped any other way. He's a hero. And he needs your help. This new story changes your emotion, which in turn changes how you act. You may call the police, but for a different reason.

You have power to change your emotions before they change you. However, you must learn to change your story. You have to reexamine the facts, identify the story you told yourself, and then tell a new story.

Stephen Covey, in his book *The Seven Habits of Highly Effective People* gives a profound illustration of changing your emotions:

> I remember a mini-paradigm shift I experienced one Sunday morning on a subway in New York. People were sitting quietly—some reading newspapers, some lost in thought, some resting with their eyes closed. It was a calm, peaceful scene. Then suddenly, a man and his children entered the subway car. The children were so loud and rambunctious that instantly the whole climate changed.
>
> The man sat down next to me and closed his eyes, apparently oblivious to the situation. The children were yelling back and forth,

throwing things, even grabbing people's papers. It was very disturbing. And yet, the man sitting next to me did nothing.

It was difficult not to feel irritated. I could not believe that he could be so insensitive to let his children run wild like that and do nothing about it, taking no responsibility at all. It was easy to see that everyone else on the subway felt irritated, too. So finally, with what I felt was unusual patience and restraint, I turned to him and said, "Sir, your children are really disturbing a lot of people. I wonder if you couldn't control them a little more?"

The man lifted his gaze as if to come to a consciousness of the situation for the first time and said softly, "Oh, you're right. I guess I should do something about it. We just came from the hospital where their mother died about an hour ago. I don't know what to think, and I guess they don't know how to handle it either."

Can you imagine what I felt at that moment? My paradigm shifted. Suddenly I *saw* things differently, and because I *saw* things differently, I *thought* differently, I *felt* differently, I *behaved* differently. My irritation vanished. I didn't have to worry about controlling my attitude or my behavior; my heart was filled with the man's pain. Feelings of sympathy and compassion flowed freely. "Your wife just died? Oh, I'm so sorry. Can you tell me about it? What can I do to help?" Everything changed in an instant.[1]

Let's walk through a more common example that involves Women's Weakness.

Melissa had told her husband, Jerry, a thousand times to shut the garage door after he pulled in. It was so embarrassing when he left it open and all the neighbors could see their messy garage. Most of the mess was a lot of *her* unfinished projects she keeps meaning to "get around to." He forgot again today. It had been at least an hour when she had to go to the garage for something, only to find the garage door wide open and her husband standing there with the neighbors. Mrs. Bailey was looking right at the mess as Melissa walked over to say hello.

The facts are simple: Her husband is home and the garage door is open. The Baileys are eyeing the chaos. Can you imagine the story that she starts to tell herself? Especially in light of her natural tendency to think less of herself? "He *knows* I hate the garage door open, yet he doesn't close it. . . . He doesn't care. And now the Baileys know what a slob I am, and it's Jerry's fault.

Can you guess what emotion that story is going to create in Melissa? Now she's being pulled into the funnel. She's going to get more and more discouraged as all her flaws come rushing at her.

But let's stop and reexamine the facts. Is there any other reason he might have left the garage door open? Is there really any hard evidence that he doesn't care or that the Baileys are even noticing the mess?

Let's suppose that Melissa, after reexamining the evidence, changes her story. She concludes that her husband *does* care about her. He was just in a hurry and forgot to close the garage door. He *is* a bit forgetful but is also so sweet.

She also could have changed her emotions quickly by using CSG. When she starts to do her Self-Scan, she immediately has to tell herself the truth: that her home is indeed quite orderly and clean—this is the garage, and it's on their to-do list to clean it out. What did she fear? Rejection by the Baileys? Mrs. Bailey doesn't have a mean bone in her body. And her husband, being a guy, doesn't even notice the mess in the garage. Quickly, (Go!) she runs in the house and brings out a small plate of cookies and gives them to the Baileys.

Now a different emotion fills her heart. Funnel avoided.

The key is to be brave enough to reexamine the evidence; to question your story; and then to tell a new story, one that brings the emotions you want to feel. It is often surprising to people to confront the story they told themselves in light of what they actually saw and heard. It may help, as you reexamine the evidence, to ask yourself, "What is the most logical reason a person might do or say that?" In our experience, our first interpretation of the facts is usually incomplete and incorrect. A reexamination usually brings greater understanding and leads to much better stories.

There are two particular stories that you need to change. The first is the story to tell yourself about you. You are not as bad as you lead yourself to believe. That story needs to change. The second is the story you tell yourself about others, especially other women. They are not as beautiful, or as organized, or as whatever as you think. They are just like you, with their own personal struggles and shortcomings. That story also needs to change. Many of the subsequent tools listed in this book will help you change those two stories.

WE DARE YOU

The next time you find yourself feeling an emotion that you would like to change, change your story. Reexamine what you actually saw and heard and separate that from your conclusion. Is your story the most likely or most logical? Did you jump to conclusions that are just not true? If so, change your story and notice how that new story changes your emotions.

NOTE

1. Stephen R. Covey, *The 7 Habits of Highly Effective People* (New York: Simon & Schuster, 1989), 30-31.

twelve

MAKE UP A STORY

In the preceding chapter, we talked about changing your emotions by reexamining the facts and then changing your story. However, sometimes it's just easier to make up a story, one that creates positive emotions to replace the negative ones. We have received some resistance to this idea. Many women push back and state that they don't feel comfortable making up a story that isn't true, just to make them feel a particular emotion. However, the reality is that they are probably doing that anyway, so why not choose a story that makes you happy instead?

Perhaps the following experience will illustrate our point. This is a story told to us during a focus group that included six women:

Haley was an intelligent, well-spoken administrative assistant for a large bank. Her boss was one of seven vice presidents for the bank. A special meeting was called in which all seven vice presidents were told to bring their administrative assistants with them. Haley knew this was somewhat unusual, but she was excited and intrigued, as were the other assistants she knew.

The meeting was nearly three hours long on a Friday afternoon. It was conducted by the president of the bank; he was soliciting ideas from the entire group regarding a solution to a major problem with one of their internal systems. At the end of the meeting, the president asked them all to think more about the problem and solutions and to email him personally if they had any more thoughts and ideas.

Haley went home. The next day she had several ideas pop into her head regarding Friday's meeting. She sat down at the computer and spent almost three hours writing her thoughts and some interesting solutions to the problems that were discussed in the meeting. She hit the "send" key, and off it went to the president of the bank.

That night she got a personal email back from the bank president, thanking her and telling her that her ideas were excellent and he would suggest they be implemented immediately. She was thrilled to think that he even read it, let alone that he said it was excellent work.

Now comes the interesting part. Two days later she was sitting in our discussion group. Haley then told us the whole story about the meeting and her email. Then she said the following: "That night, after I read the email from the president of the bank, I started thinking that there were thirteen other people in that meeting with me. I'll bet they all sent him emails too, and most of them have college degrees, even some of the assistants. How can I compete with *that*? I only have an associate's degree. I'll bet Sarah sent him a ten-page email with incredible ideas. And Mr. Johnson graduated from Harvard. Like I can compete with that!"

Haley told us that after she thought about the whole thing, she was embarrassed that she had even sent the email and wished she hadn't sent it in at all.

So we analyzed her story. We told her, "Haley, what if you had just changed your story?"

"What do you mean 'change my story'?"

We told her that she *could* have said to herself, "Wow, the president of the bank said I did excellent work. That's really amazing, and maybe, just maybe, I'm the *only* one from that meeting that sent him any ideas. That's cool!"

Haley then blurted out, "But I'm not going to lie to myself. I don't know if I *was* the *only* one."

Then we caught her in her own trap. Even some of the other

women in our group saw what was happening. Haley didn't want to make up a "positive" story *that wasn't true* (according to her) so she made up a "negative" story *that wasn't true.*

"Haley, think about it! You made up your story—the story that the others in the meeting had probably all sent emails that were so much better than yours, and that you really had nothing to offer in comparison to the Harvard guy. You made that up. It wasn't true —it's what you came up with in your own head. Why can't you just change that story?"

Haley didn't get it. She couldn't see that she had the *choice* of which "story" she was going to use. She made up the one about how everybody else had better ideas than hers. Couldn't she have just as easily caught herself in the act, changed her story, which would then have changed a few chemicals in her brain and given her a brighter outlook about the whole situation?

It wasn't until our next meeting that Haley could actually see what she had done in retrospect. At the time she told us about the incident, she was too emotionally wrapped up in "her story" to be able to see that there was any other conclusion. She didn't want to "tell herself a lie" but she already had.

Why not put a positive spin on it instead of the negative spin. It's up to us. We write our own stories all day long, so change your story—even if you have to make one up.

We feel it is critical that you understand this tool. Do you see how you make stories up all day long? We all do it. Our Inner Critic helps us make up negative stories. Our true Inner Voice can help us make up a different, constructive story. Tell Icy to get lost. You are in charge of your stories, even when you are triggered so badly you could scream.

WE DARE YOU

Think back to a recent experience you had in which you told yourself a story that resulted in negative emotions. Now make up a new story, one that completely changes the way you feel about that experience. If you truly examine both stories, is the one you "made up" any more or less likely than the one you told yourself originally? Now do this the next time you face a negative emotion. Why not tell yourself a positive story?

thirteen

THE FINE ART OF PROCRASTINATION

Sooner or later every woman must ask herself if she has Women's Weakness. We have interviewed many women and talked to them about the concepts behind this seemingly inherent weakness (the propensity of women to be self-deprecating and sometimes even self-loathing). After hearing it, and reflecting upon it, these women invariably say, "I have it."

One woman we spoke with denied that she suffered from this malady of being so hard on herself or of constantly comparing herself to other women. In other words, she didn't think she had Women's Weakness. This was a beautiful woman in her late thirties. She was probably five foot ten, had perfectly styled blonde highlighted hair, and weighed around 125 pounds. She was dressed in a gorgeous red outfit and wearing tastefully chosen jewelry. Her high heels were amazing. She looked like she was right out of some "modern woman" magazine. We chatted for a little while about her life. She was the president of a large women's organization and lived a very busy life with her family.

Here are the basics from our conversation about Women's Weakness:

RJ: *So that is the concept behind what we call Women's Weakness. Do you see it in yourself?*

Michelle: *Actually, no, I don't—I really don't have a problem with that kind of thing.*

RJ: *Oh? Okay. Well, then, let me ask you a question, if I may. Let's suppose that tomorrow you go to the doctor for the results of a blood test and the doctor tells you that they found something and want to check it out further. You are sent in for an MRI, and it comes back to reveal that you have a small tumor in your pituitary gland. This means that over the next six to twelve months you are going to gain fifty to sixty pounds—and right now there is nothing you can do about it. How would you feel?*

(At this point she literally put her hands up to her face as if someone had just splashed ice-cold water in her face.)

Michelle: *Are you kidding me? I would just die if I gained any weight at all! I pride myself in keeping my body trim and fit. I watch what I eat all the time. That would just do me in if I gained even ten pounds!*

RJ: *Well, I can see I hit a sensitive nerve there. Let me ask you this: let's say right now you weigh 175 pounds and you go on a diet and lose fifty pounds. How would you feel about yourself then?*

Michelle: *I'd feel great! I feel best right at 125 pounds.*

RJ: *But don't you see what's happening here?*

Michelle: *What?*

RJ: *You are basing how you feel about yourself on how you look. That's a very slippery slope to be on in your life. That means as long as your weight is down, you're okay. When it goes up, you're not okay. That's basing your worth on how other people see you, not on your intrinsic worth as a woman. Do you think God establishes your worth on how much you weigh or how good you look on the outside?*

Michelle: *But I don't want to be huge!*

RJ: *Why not?*

Michelle: *What would other people think of me?*

(All of a sudden she realized what she was saying and just stared at me.)

RJ: *Are you seeing it now? What you are saying is that if you keep your weight down, then you're worth more than if your weight goes up. You could do that in all areas of your life. If your children do extremely well in school, you're a great mom. If one of your children is flunking ninth grade math, you're a terrible mother and* you are worth less—or worthless. *Do you see how easy it is to play that game? That's all part of Women's Weakness. You see, it's all based on our perceptions of what we think others might be thinking about us.*

Michelle: *Wow, I never thought of it that way. I guess, given the right set of circumstances, I really do have Women's Weakness.*

RJ: *Wouldn't it be interesting to see what you would be telling yourself about yourself after you had gained even ten pounds? Or what kind of lies would be going through your mind about what kind of mother you are if your sixteen-year-old daughter came home from school one day and told you that she is pregnant?*

Michelle: *Yeah . . . I can see how I really do base my self-worth on my looks. Ouch. That sounds so shallow.*

RJ: *Don't be too hard on yourself. Almost all women get caught up in this trap. I don't think you can go through junior high school without getting your first real dose of Women's Weakness, because the world is set up to question our worth at every step.*

Michelle: *But I don't want my own daughters to have to go through this.*

RJ: *That's why you have to teach them these principles now. I have always joked that you women compare yourselves to the Joan of Arc or Mother Teresa and feel inferior. We men compare ourselves to someone like Hitler and come off smelling like a rose!*

And then there was Margaret. Margaret said that she struggled with Women's Weakness for most of her life but no longer deals with it. It had been painful and made her so tired, but she didn't do it to herself anymore.

Margaret was eighty-four.

Don't wait that long.

PROCRASTINATION AND RATIONALIZATION: THE GREAT STUMBLING BLOCKS OF WOMEN'S WEAKNESS

Women face a problem. Their self-demeaning thoughts have become habit. Habits become, over time, addictions. So we become addicted to thinking negative thoughts about ourselves. Sometimes it's automatic. It just happens. We've always done it; we probably always will. Unless . . .

Contemplate the following quotation by Robert Louis Stevenson: "You cannot run away from a weakness; you must sometime fight it out or perish—and if this be so, why not now, and where you stand?"

Facing our weaknesses and our bad habits requires honesty with self. So let us get to the point of this chapter: rationalization and its evil twin, procrastination.

Our excuses need to be exposed for what they are: illusions. Most women tell us they have been fighting harmful thoughts about themselves since probably junior high school (who can survive junior high without major wounds to the psyche—either inflicted by others or self-inflicted)? If *you* have been fighting this warped thinking most of your life, then isn't it time to finally "fight it out . . . and if this be so, why not now and where you stand?"

Let's look at the most common excuses for not doing what you know you should (all of which have a dishonest defense attached to them):

- Not enough time
- Lack of resources
- Don't know how to change
- Don't have the capability to change
- I've tried before—it didn't work
- I'm too old (or too young) to make a significant change
- I cannot control my circumstances (poor luck, and so on) "If it weren't for . . ."

Is it more important to momentarily avoid a hit to your ego or to finally create the life and experiences you've always wanted? It takes time and work to stop rationalizing and procrastinating, but it really all begins with a decision. When that commitment is made to stop using the above excuses and when the choice to stop justifying your inaction is genuine and sincere, then the next action step can follow.

How do we "expose" our excuses?

The first thing we need to have you do may require a small amount of effort. We realize that reading this book requires effort in and of itself—but in order to actually *apply* what you are learning here will now require you to get out a pen and paper and actually do more than just *reading* this book. This is a moment of self-honesty.

So if you *really* want to change your thinking about yourself, get out a paper and pen right now and do the following exercise; it will pay off.

Now, look at the seven bullet points on the previous page and determine which ones apply to you. "Not enough time"? Maybe that is one of your big ones. "Too old"? Write it down. "Tried it before"? Include it, too! If all seven apply, write them all down, and leave a space below each one.

Did you do it? Be honest. We suggest if you don't have time to write it down now, put the book down and don't read any further until you can sit with paper and pen and complete this exercise.

Okay. Let's move on. What you are going to do now is expose your excuses. Under each excuse on your paper, write down the reasons you use to explain that justification. Here's an example:

"I'm too old to make any significant change."
- I'm forty-three years old. Too much of my life has gone by and I'm too set in my ways to change. It's not worth it—I should have started when I was twenty. You can't teach an old dog new tricks.

"I've tried before—it didn't work."
- Years ago, I tried one of those self-improvement programs

and nothing ever came of it. I know others who have tried to change—like my sister—and she saw no improvement. If I try again and fail, I'll just be more depressed about myself.

So for each of your bullet points you are going to explain your thinking, reasoning, or excuse for why you can't do it. Start writing!

Now what we want you to do is confront each of the points you have written down with objective facts and concrete evidence that your excuses are merely that: empty reasons without foundation. You must shine the light of truth on each of these reasons so you are clear in your mind that they simply are *not* true. The truth will indeed make you free—free from the crippling habit of procrastination and rationalization that you have been letting run your life up to this point.

Again, it's a matter of honesty. But without ever examining your reasons for your inaction and procrastination, you will continue to avoid the changes you desire.

The final step in this exercise is going to allow you to reverse this pattern in your life. Each excuse you wrote down can be absolutely refuted, thus removing them from your default setting.

Now comes the fun part, but it will require you to do some creative thinking and writing. Go back to each excuse, one by one, give proof of why that excuse can be fully refuted; why that particular excuse or justification that you cited is, in reality, a lie. Here's an example from above:

"I'm too old to make any significant change."
- I'm forty-three years old. Too much of my life has gone by and I'm too set in my ways to change. It's not worth it—I should have started when I was twenty. You can't teach an old dog new tricks.

- **Refuted:** "I'm too old? Are you kidding me? At forty-three years old, if I live the average lifespan of a woman I've got another forty or fifty years left to work on this. Think of what could be done in just one year if I really concentrated on overcoming my low self-worth issues. Time is really on my side here! And another thing:

with maturity comes a greater ability to understand, and I'll be more patient with myself and my mistakes as I get older. There are no mandatory time restrictions when it comes to changing my thought patterns. *Any age* is the correct age to make a change in my rotten thinking about myself. And I've seen people older than I am that have made incredible changes in their lives. I even read that most people make their fortunes *after* they are sixty years old."

Do you see how she found at least five or six good reasons to undermine her previously written excuses? Now she is using her mind to find all the reasons why her excuses are not true. Let's do another example:

"I've tried before—it didn't work."
- Years ago I tried one of those self-improvement programs and nothing ever came of it. I know others who have tried to change—like my sister—and she saw no improvement. I've tried everything. If I try again and fail, I'll just be more depressed about myself.
- **Refuted:** "Yeah, okay, I did do that one program before. I really didn't try very hard and I didn't do what the program suggested. My sister? I am not my sister! That's so lame I can't believe I wrote that! And 'I've tried everything'? Oh, really? I tried one. (I tend to exaggerate when it comes to this kind of thing.) This says nothing about what I can really do if I set my mind to it. And I *do* know that others have set out to change things in their lives and have done a magnificent job of it. Failing one time does not a habit make. Scientifically I have read that the brain can change habits—so I've got science backing me up on this. Failing once is failing once, nothing more.

There are at least five refutations of "I've tried before—it didn't work" in her lineup. She sees what lies she has been telling herself. Notice, though, that it didn't really come into view for her until she *wrote it down*.

Take the time now to write down your points that will refute or prove wrong each of the excuses you are using. This writing exercise is critical if you want to make permanent changes. Do it!

This exercise is to prove to your mind that there is no reasonable excuse for inaction. But you must convince yourself of this idea, and that is why writing it down on paper forces your mind to confront these issues head on. It forces your brain to go past the superficial and search for other reasons. Please, don't read further in this book until you have completed these writing exercises. They can uncover epiphanies!

(Notice that we didn't fill this book with a bunch of blank pages with lines on them for you to write on. We asked women if they really would write in a book and 100 percent said "no." "Why not?" we asked. Because they were afraid someone would get hold of the book twenty years later and read what they wrote! Okay, okay, we get it (although that person reading it twenty years later may be a grand-daughter with low self-worth that really needs to read it!). So go grab a notebook and start writing!

This is part of your *training*. Don't try. Train!

If you are *still* struggling with actually *doing* some of these exercises in this book, we understand. As with all actions, you can break it down to a "cost vs. benefits" analysis. What are the costs in your life for doing nothing about your low self-image? Compare those costs to the benefits in your life if you *did* put forth even a small amount of effort. There is no comparison, so stop procrastinating and start doing. Buy a spiral notebook and start writing. There will be more on that later.

Two choices exist:

"Don't just sit there—do something!" Or, "Don't just do something—sit there." Well?

WE DARE YOU

We dare you to go back in this chapter and examine your rationalizations for not changing, for not using the tools in this book. What could happen in your life if you stopped procrastinating change and really took action? Have you memorized CSG like we dared you to at the end of chapter 6? Examine which of the rationalizations illustrated in this chapter you are using daily that hold you back.

fourteen

Mirror, Mirror on the Wall

Quiz question: What is the most powerful drug known to humanity?

Answer: According to the famous author Rudyard Kipling, "I am by nature a dealer in words, and words are the most powerful drug known to humanity."

So if words are so powerful, then we must change our words, for those words floating through our hearts and minds are the key to change. We all tend to be careless and sloppy with the words we choose regarding ourselves. We can change our entire world by selecting the right words. But again, we sometimes lie to ourselves about ourselves. As Socrates said so wisely, "False words are not only evil in themselves, but they infect the soul with evil."

Words are our weapons, whether we use them on someone else, or on ourselves. When we try to be "good" in our behavior toward others, we really try hard not to say bad things about our neighbor. But when it comes to ourselves, we can be so mean. It comes down to self-acceptance.

In our focus groups, women have told us that one of the hardest things they could ever do is accept themselves. After digesting that over time, we decided to give a few women a homework assignment. Here was the assignment:

"Three times per day we want you to look in the mirror and say the following three times: *I accept myself unconditionally right now.* After a couple weeks, report on your experience." A simple assignment. Or maybe not . . .

Andrea's experience:

When you first told me what I had to say to myself in the mirror, I thought it was kind of silly, plus I thought it was no big deal . . . until the next morning when I tried it right after I got out of the shower. I stood there with my towel wrapped around me, staring at myself. I looked first at my wrinkly skin. Then I looked at my dark roots. Then my abs. Then I thought, "Okay, this isn't gonna work" and I started to cry. I couldn't say the words you wanted me to say. They wouldn't come out. I didn't try it again for two days because I was so mad.

The next time I tried it was at night. My husband was out of town on business. I stood in front of the bathroom mirror again, with all my clothes and makeup on (that way I seemed a little bit more acceptable). I just stood there for probably a whole minute staring into my own eyes. Somewhere I heard that "the eyes are the windows to the soul." As I stared into them, I saw myself as a little lost girl. I started to cry again, so I went and lay on my bed to get control of myself. Why was this so hard? Why so awkward and uncomfortable?

I guess this assignment wasn't so silly after all. I was truly learning something about myself that I needed to learn. So I went back to the mirror with the attitude of being a friend to myself. After looking into my eyes again, and seeing that little girl, I squeaked out the words I accept myself unconditionally right now. Then I said it slowly two more times.

Frankly, it was painful. I could actually feel my heart beating fast. But I felt something more. Even though I said the words hesitantly and cautiously, I felt a small amount of peace. I felt tranquil; I guess is the best word to describe it. Maybe warm inside. I really didn't feel as hypocritical as I thought I would.

The next morning I got up, showered, got the kids off to school, and walked down the hall to the kids' bathroom. I bent down to pick up their clothes. As I stood up, I caught myself in the mirror. I stared into my eyes again. I thought it weird that I had never really ever looked deeply into my own eyes, but there were so many stories in there. So I said the six simple words again: I accept myself unconditionally right now. I didn't cry!

The funny thing is, I started looking forward to my little "ritual in the mirror" three times a day. After several days of doing this a strange thing started happening: I could feel myself being so much less critical of myself. I wasn't so hard on me. I started feeling a little worthier of being me. This was very peculiar for me, because I have always tended to be a super-perfectionist, which makes life pretty hard when you never are perfect.

Thank you for the assignment to write about my experience. I am doing it at least three times per day—sometimes I use the rearview mirror in my car to look into my eyes. Seems like each time I do it I get stronger and I learn something about myself. I have learned that I'm okay.

That is the ultimate "okay." Robert Holden, PhD, in his book *Happiness Now* writes,

> *Without self-acceptance, you are always hiding.*
> *With self-acceptance, your spirit is gliding.*

We think that Andrea's mirror ritual started her down the path of spiritual gliding, even soaring. She began learning the truth about herself, from herself, and it made her free. Every woman, every man, every child on this earth deserves this emergence. Holden concluded,

"The greatest pain of all is the fear that happiness might somehow elude us forever; the greatest joy of all is the realization that the potential for happiness is available to us now and always."[1]

I accept myself unconditionally right now. Notice the word "unconditionally." That means without reservation. Without any qualifications. If you really want to get sassy, you may, as Holden suggests, add this line:

And I am completely adorable!

Gutsy? Brash? Maybe so, but we dare you to try it and see what feelings come up. There is nobody else on this earth like you. You are unique and therefore adorable.

IT'S ALL IN YOUR HEAD

One of the points we are trying to make is this: whatever idea you hold in your mind over time about yourself is exactly what you will create in your life. Notice Andrea's comment,

*After several days of doing this a strange thing started happening: I could
feel myself being so much less critical of myself. I wasn't so hard on me. I
started feeling a little worthier of being me.*

Repetition is the key. That is part of the training we have talked
about. If you merely say, "Well, I've tried to tell myself things like that
about myself—but it just didn't take." That again is the difference
between "trying" and "training."

Training is saying "I accept myself unconditionally right now"
three times per day in the mirror.

Training is using *Confront—Scan—Go* every time you stand at
the edge of the "funnel."

Training is changing your story.

You see, you can read the words on this page and never let them
affect you. Or you can let the words pierce you enough to get into the
training mode. As stated above, words are your weapons. If negative
words about yourself bathe your mind all day long, that's what you'll
get in your life. But we have given you powerful tools to use to build
a new way of thinking for you.

The majority of people get out of bed each morning, look in the
mirror, and are not pleased with what they see. So, for the rest of the
day they beat themselves up mentally. Let us ask you this: if you had
a companion with you 24/7 that was shouting that negative stuff in
your face, you wouldn't permit that, would you? Oh yes, you would,
because that is *you*. You can train that out of yourself. You MUST
train that out of yourself.

Our brains have been programmed from when we were children
to seek the lowest level of uncontrolled thinking. But if we continu-
ously plant uplifting, ennobling thoughts in our minds many times
throughout the day, little by little our uncontrolled thinking becomes
a little more restrained. We are not as likely to berate ourselves when
we do something dumb.

The first step is self-acceptance. This will eventually lead to self-
love and a love of all others in our lives.

DEALING WITH OTHERS IN OUR LIVES

Jenna was a hard-working, capable attorney in a large law firm. She had the respect of her bosses and coworkers, except for one. She couldn't figure out what she had ever done to Jackie. Jackie was just plain rude to her. She obviously didn't like Jenna. One time she came over to Jenna's office, threw a binder on the desk, and said, "This is *your* responsibility, not mine!" She stomped off without saying anything else. Jenna sat there bewildered.

Another time several of the attorneys were eating lunch together in the break room. The subject of cars came up when Jackie said, "Jenna, how can you stand to drive that thing you drive? You should get a *real car* someday." Everyone laughed, and the conversation shifted to other things. Jenna was hurt. Not being the assertive type, she didn't want to confront Jackie, so she just let it fester.

As Jenna was driving home that evening, she was halfway between being angry and being sad because of Jackie's words. Jenna happened to be listening to a radio talk show with a psychologist being interviewed. We'll call him Dr. Mike.

Here's what Jenna heard:

Interviewer: So, Dr. Mike, we're happy to have you in the studio today to talk about interpersonal relationships! Thank you for coming. You have some interesting views on this subject.

Dr. Mike: Thanks for having me. Yes, I do have some different things to share with your listeners, especially those who struggle with any particular person in their lives who doesn't like them.

Interviewer: What do you mean?

Dr. Mike: Well, somewhere along the line in our lives, we all have to deal with someone who just seems to have it out for us. They don't treat us well at all. This could even be our spouse at times! But mostly it's an acquaintance of some kind, or someone that we have to work around.

[This caught Jenna's attention immediately]

Interviewer: Yeah, I can think of a couple people in my life, one in particular in high school, and another one at my first job.

Dr. Mike: We're going to run into them everywhere. My point is that they are thrown in our paths to make us better people.

Interviewer: *Better* people? How do you mean that?

Dr. Mike: It makes us better if we realize one important thing. If someone doesn't like me, it tells me something really revealing about them. Do you know what it tells me?

Interviewer: I don't know.

Dr. Mike: If someone doesn't like me, it tells me that they don't like themselves, because if they really liked themselves, they would like me.

Interviewer: I'm not sure I follow you.

Dr. Mike: Look, if someone treats you badly, what do you know? You know that they must be unhappy with themselves. People who love themselves and are happy with their lives don't go around ragging on others—they're comfortable in their own skin and don't need to bring you down to feel good.

Interviewer: Whoa! That's heavy stuff. So you're saying that if someone doesn't like me or treat me well, it's because that's really how they feel about themselves?

Dr. Mike: Exactly. So how can I tell if you like yourself? Obviously—you'll like me!

Interviewer: So then if someone treats me rudely, it's not because I've done anything wrong or deserve to be treated poorly. It says nothing about me but tells me a lot about them. Is that the idea?

Dr. Mike: That's it exactly. Jesus said, "Thou shalt love thy neighbor as thyself." In other words, you'll only be able to love your neighbor to the extent that you love yourself. If you don't like or love yourself, you won't really like or love your neighbor.

Interviewer: Wow! That's something that every child in this world needs to know as they grow up. You can't make it through junior high school without getting treated badly by other kids. If our children could only catch that vision that when someone is picking on them, it tells them a lot about what that other person thinks about him- or herself, and *nothing* about who *your children* themselves really are. That's very empowering!

Jenna sat there in her car, dumbfounded, "You mean that the way Jackie is treating me at work says nothing about me? It's just a reflection of how she feels about herself? You've got to be kidding me. That explains so much. She must not like herself to be treating me the way she does. *It's not about me! And actually she tends to treat almost everyone like she treated me.*

Key Concept: How someone feels about another person is only a reflection of how he or she feels about him- or herself.

Do you see how empowering that knowledge is? It is liberating, at the very least. It releases us from the tyranny of our thoughts about ourselves if we can realize that if so-and-so doesn't like us for some known or unknown reason, it's because he or she doesn't really understand or love him- or herself yet. But it has nothing to do with me!

Consider this scenario:

Molly comes home from work and immediately starts fixing dinner. About ten minutes later Dennis gets home and walks in from the garage. Molly says, "Hi, Honey. How was your day?"

Dennis says nothing but hangs his coat up with a frown on his face, walks through the kitchen still without saying a word, and heads upstairs to the bedroom.

Fifteen minutes later, he comes down and is still silent. Molly inquires, "Is everything okay? You seem a little quiet. What's wrong?"

Dennis snaps back, "Nothing's wrong! Why does there have to be something *wrong*?" and he walks out to the garage.

So naturally, Molly starts searching in her mind for something she did wrong. She starts heading into darkness. She questions her value as a wife because "why would he treat me like that if I were the kind of woman that he needs? I'm obviously not meeting his needs." And so she quickly steps into weakness and out of strength.

What Molly really needs to realize is what Dr. Mike was trying to get across to his audience in the interview above. Dennis's treatment of Molly has *nothing to do with Molly* and everything to do with himself because right now Dennis doesn't like himself. He got a speeding ticket on the way home from work for driving thirty miles per hour over the speed limit. That ticket will cost them two hundred and fifty dollars—which they just can't afford right now.

Right now, Dennis *thinks* he is a bad person. So he is taking it out on Molly, and probably on the kids, or whoever else crosses his path that evening. Does getting a ticket mean Dennis is a bad person? Not at all—but that is how Dennis perceives it. If he is a bad person (in his own mind) then that means he doesn't like himself. If he doesn't like himself, at that moment he doesn't like anyone else.

The main point here is this: whenever someone treats us poorly, rudely, with contempt, or is offensive to us in any way, we know one thing for sure: it's saying nothing about us, and volumes about how they feel about themselves. We cannot emphasize the importance of this concept enough. With this insight we are freed; without it we can remain in bondage forever, always at the mercy of someone else's feelings.

We can accept ourselves unconditionally—right now!

WE DARE YOU

Go find a mirror and do the same assignment we gave the women in this chapter. Three time every day. Just do it. This is a critical part of training, not trying. Also, the next time someone is "dumping" on you, let the thought run through your head: "This is not about me. This is about her/him. She/he doesn't really feel good about her/himself. This is just a reflection of how they are feeling inside.

NOTE

1. Robert Holden, *Happiness Now!* (Carlsbad, CA: Hay House, 2007).

fifteen

THE SELF-WORTH BOONDOGGLE

As defined in the dictionary, the term "self-worth" reads: the sense of one's own value or worth as a person; self-esteem; self-respect. How do you value yourself? An interesting question indeed. This begs the question, where does my value come from? From God? From my parents and family? From my friends?

Let's look more closely at how we develop our sense of self-worth.

HOW TO CREATE FEELINGS OF LOW AND HIGH SELF-WORTH

In order to figure out how to create feelings of *high* self-worth, we must first understand where feelings of *low* self-worth come from.

We experience feelings of low self-worth when our view of ourselves is dependent on external, rather than internal, factors. True self-worth comes when we stop trying to derive our worth from "the world" and realize that true worth is an inherent trait and not something we have to earn.

The following are some of the most common contributors toward your feelings of self-worth:

Performance

1. When your house is a mess, you feel of lesser value.
2. When you gain thirty pounds, you feel inferior.
3. When you lose thirty pounds, you feel of greater value.
4. You get a promotion at work—you feel better about yourself.
5. You lose your job—and you are worth less (or worthless).
6. You have a wonderful marriage: you are worthwhile.
7. You are a divorcee—your worth goes way down.
8. Your kids are superstars at all they do—you are a good parent.
9. Your son got kicked out of high school for selling drugs—you are worthless.

As you can see, it doesn't make a difference whether you use the positive emotions to feel good about yourself or you use the negative emotions to feel of lesser value, because either way you are depending on the world (or an external source) to give you value. This should not be the case! Value or worth is intrinsic.

Possessions

1. You bought a new luxury car—your sense of self-worth goes way up.
2. You drive an old car with a few dents—you're not as good as the neighbor with the luxury car.
3. You have a huge, lovely home with all the trimmings—naturally you feel so much better about yourself.
4. Your house is the poorest on the block.
5. You have a whole new wardrobe so you can use these feelings to create your higher self-worth.

Opinions/Honors

1. You run with an affluent crowd. This makes you look good to those who have less than you do.
2. You are the president of the local PTA. This helps determines your worth.

3. If others look up to my chosen profession (or look down on my profession), these feelings can determine value.
4. If I serve others, I can base my value on that; if they appreciate my service, I will continue. If not, I will quit.
5. If I never graduated from college, I can use these feelings to determine my value, or I have a PhD, so my value is much greater.

These are all different types of performance. These are all extrinsic values, and have nothing to do with who you are. We are not on this earth to prove our worth. That is predetermined. We should never use the bad feelings that come from poor performance to put ourselves down. Answer these questions in your own mind:

*   Is your internal worth really based on how much education you have?
*   Is your value tied to your net worth?
*   Do you love yourself more if you weigh less?
*   Does your worth hang in the balance according to how good your hair looks on a particular day?
*   If you gave a speech, and you didn't do as well as you thought you should have, does that put a big dent in your self-worth?

Now you might ask, "Wait a minute. What if I really *did* give a good speech? Can't I feel good about that?"

Certainly you can feel good about it. But the difference we are trying to show here is that there is a difference in *feeling good* about your speech—and basing your *worth* on your speech. What happens then the next time you give a speech and you do poorly? If your self-worth is tied to your performance, now you have just gone down a few rungs on the self-worth ladder. Now that's a bad program. To sum up:

WORTH IS NOT EQUAL TO PERFORMANCE!

It's natural to be elated about my performance when it's good, but that is going into the "danger zone" because we should *never* use these feelings to create good feelings about who we are and what value we

151

have. When we use our performance to help us feel good about ourselves, we are setting ourselves up to get hooked by the world.

That means when my performance is up, my worth is up. When my performance is down, my worth is down. Again, this is a slippery slope to be on. We need to recognize that no matter what our performance is (or our children's performance or the opinions of others or how much our net worth is or isn't) *our self-worth or value never changes. It is constant.* No matter what we do in this life, our worth is perpetual. There are no contingencies on that fact. There are no conditions that will ever change that.

Now that you know how to create feelings of low self-worth, you can quickly start seeing in your daily activities and conversations when you are playing "the game" of dependency on the world to make you feel good—or bad—about yourself. Once you are aware of these issues, you can spot them so much more easily every day. If someone rejects you, you can look past it now, knowing that his or her rejection of you has *nothing* to do with who you *really are.* You can treat yourself with awe and respect. You then refuse to give your agency to that person. He or she has no control over you because your worth is founded on the inner truth—not lies from the world's opinions. In a previous chapter we talked about "Comparison Sickness"—a weakness that is a frontal assault on every woman's worth.

When we realize that our worth is intrinsic, and that it will never change no matter what we do, then there is then no need for comparing; there is no need for judging others. If we value ourselves, we have no need to look outside ourselves for validation. There is nothing to prove. We are who we are and we don't need to have it reconfirmed to us every day from someone else in our lives. We don't need outside sources to "justify our existence." Our validation comes from an internal source—that divine voice within us that *never* lies to us. Deep down inside there is that internal true opinion whispering the truth to you.

The problem is that we get so easily hooked by the world around us that sometimes it obliterates the truth inside us and we lose our way. Our compass stops working and we can't figure out which way is "true north" anymore. But we can train ourselves to stop getting hooked. The tools we give you in this book can train you back to "true north." You *must* confront the lies. You *must* scan yourself for the truth and hidden fears, and then you *must* go. It works if you'll use it. Tools left lying on the workbench never finish the job.

WE DARE YOU

We dare you to go back through chapter 15 and then teach these new concepts to someone else in your life. It's been said that the best way to really "own" an important concept is to teach it to someone else. It is critical that you see how you have been basing your self-worth on incorrect ideas. This goes all the way back to your default settings. Go find someone and teach!

sixteen

You Need a Buddy

In the US Army there is an effective program used to help protect soldiers in times of conflict and war. It is simply referred to as "Battle Buddies."

The concept is this: whenever a soldier is training for battle, he or she is assigned a "battle buddy" that they will look out for and stick with. That buddy will do the same for that soldier.

We suggest that you are going through a war as you are trying to overcome your old ways of self-contempt, low self-worth, and poor self-image. It can be a daily battle due to the fact that you have been doing it to yourself since you were a child. You need a person in your life that you can have as your buddy—a change agent that will be your confidant. It will make the process of getting out of your funnels much easier.

A synonym for your "battle buddy" would be the term *confidant*. A confidant is someone whom you can trust with private, personal, and sensitive information about yourself. We all need at least one confidant in our lives, but as you are going through this transformation process of changing how you feel about yourself, you must have a confidant: a friend, spouse, sister, or someone you can share this book with. Whether *your* confidant needs help or not with his or her own self-worth, you can talk to this person about the concepts outlined in the book. After a self-worth attack, talk it through with this person.

Choosing a trustworthy person to share your innermost thoughts with can be a delicate task. Unfortunately, the capability to keep a secret is simply not a quality that everyone possesses. If you are going to disclose the details of your personal life, it's a good idea to take the time to consider whether your secret will be safe. Before you share your feelings with a friend, ask yourself if he or she has been responsible in the past. If that person is best described as irresponsible and thoughtless, think twice before sharing your ideas and feelings as you strive to change your views of yourself. A friend who regularly gossips about others is also a poor choice to share your feelings with. The best confidant is a friend who is both sensitive and compassionate.

Your first step in this process, after you have selected a person you *think* might be a good "battle buddy" is to have him or her read this book and then talk with you about how he or she feels about what he or she has read. If this person cannot identify with the feelings of low self-worth, maybe he or she is not the best confidant you could find. This person may be a person that suffers from Woman's Weakness the same way you do. It may be an older woman who has been through the same battles you've been through, but has won some of the crucial battles and could help you see things more clearly. Your confidant may be your spouse or partner.

As you talk with your confidant about what is in this book, it won't take long for you to see if this person relates to these concepts. If the messages in the book resonate with him or her, they'll probably resonate with you. You must feel comfortable with this person.

It's great to work with someone on your level who has no ulterior motives, no ax to grind, and can tell it as it is.

It's really empowering to work through things with someone who is a peer—it gives your confidence a real boost to start with a sticky problem (like low self-worth) and then find that with a bit of support and encouragement, you can see improvement. Go back through this book with your buddy and find the areas you really need to work on. Maybe your buddy has other ideas. Maybe your buddy has been through it too. You can laugh together as you read the many scenarios we have put in the book, knowing that you are not alone in the battle against Women's Weakness.

As Norman Vincent Peale once said, "Action is a great restorer of confidence"

As you find a buddy that can be your confidant, it will build your confidence at a much faster rate than if you do this all by yourself. This is a case of synergy, where 1+1=3. You are each other's sounding boards. You can also hold each other accountable. If Icy gets to you, tell your buddy. Have her play the role of Icy (Inner Critic) and you practice talking back to that inner critic. You'll be surprised at how effective role play can be.

If you caught yourself playing the martyr to your husband or partner, role play it. What could you have said differently so you didn't have to be the martyr?

You find yourself in a group of women that you greatly admire. As the conversation goes on, you catch yourself going into comparison mode, and you are standing at the edge of the self-deprecation funnel. Tell your buddy about the thoughts that were racing through your mind.

She can hold you accountable by asking, "Why didn't you Scan yourself right then and there? Did you confront your thoughts? Why not? What's your excuse? You *know* it helped you the last time you did it! You need to train harder!"

The next week you call your buddy to report a success. "I went into McDonald's yesterday with my kids for lunch. There was a lady in front of us in line with her kids. They were all dressed perfectly; she was a size 2 with this cute hair. My kids looked like they had just come from some halfway house, and I was in my sweats. I could feel myself sinking into comparison sickness, and then I heard Icy telling me I'm a loser mom. Then I talked back. I confronted the thoughts and went into my Scan mode. Then my 'Go' was to compliment that woman on her hair. It worked! I didn't go down the funnel. It made my whole day so much better."

Reporting successes to your buddy is critical, because it reinforces all these tools to your mind. It makes new neural pathways in your brain. It's creating new habits of thought, and that is the only way to win each of the battles in this war on low self-worth.

WE DARE YOU

Go find a "battle buddy" within the next three days. Tell them what you are doing. Give them this book and have them read it and tell them they are a trusted person in your life and you need their help for a "Life Experiment." Don't spend too much time finding "just the right person." If your first choice is not interested, great. It wasn't meant to be that person. (Remember, don't set yourselfup!) Find someone else and go for it. You both are at the beginning of a huge adventure!

seventeen

DRAGGIN', SAGGIN', AND NAGGIN':

When a Woman Doesn't Feel Good, She Never Feels Good about Herself

There is no doubt about it: when you don't feel good physically, you will never feel good about yourself. Physical affects mental, and the number one enemy is fatigue.

Draggin': physical and mental fatigue.
Saggin': losing muscle tone and putting on fat.
Naggin': irritability, PMS, anxiety, depression.

Look at this letter—an actual letter from a patient seeking help from our clinic:

> I have been putting this off for far too long, but upon the insistence of my husband, I am now pleading for help.
>
> I am not well. As you know, I have been struggling for some time. My fatigue and myriad other problems have grown worse
>
> Now months later, I am more fatigued than ever. The smallest tasks seem daunting. Getting dressed in the morning is completely exhausting. I am drained by the time the kids leave for school at 7:30. How can I be drained so early in the day? It's all I can do to stay awake with my

baby until she goes down for a nap at 8:00, at which time I head back to bed. I then sleep for 2–3 hours, accomplishing nothing and awake feeling like I'm half dead. The groggy way I feel all day is unbearable. I am semi-depressed because I feel like such a failure. I can't even clean my own house. I hire house cleaners to do my work because I'm too drained to scrub a toilet or wipe down a sink.

I have all these grand plans to be a better mom and just push through my exhaustion. But then it overtakes me and I physically and mentally cannot cope. Then I feel low about myself because I can't be the mom I want to be. And losing an extra 15 pounds? Forget about it! I have been doing hot yoga for 2 months. I stopped eating carbs, wheat, and sugar for 3 straight weeks, hoping to see a pound or two come off. Not only did I not lose anything, but I gained 2 pounds. I felt like I was going to have a breakdown.

So this past weekend I was on a girls' trip in California. We stayed up late, got up early, and spent each day on our feet for 9 hours. So why then could I manage that? Well, I figure it's because I never sat down and I had to keep going. But the minute we got into the car, on a plane, or on the Muni, I practically fainted with exhaustion and slept soundly on each transit.

On our plane ride, I was looking through the airline magazine, and came across the attached article. It just kind of spoke to me. Especially when the doctor tells the woman that her blood work is "normal." I fit each . . . symptom listed in the article, except for maybe recurring infections. Foggy brain, low (or zero) libido, difficulty losing weight, difficulty concentrating, depressed moods, tiredness after 8 hours of sleep, and on and on. Sleeping at night has become a joke. I wake up 4–5 times a night and NOT for a baby. I toss and turn, and will feel cold one minute and sweaty hot the next. I could get 8–10 hours of sleep and still be dragging the next day. I am eating protein, drinking protein shakes, doing everything I can to boost my energy, and nothing, I mean NOTHING has made the least bit of difference.

I had chalked it up to the fact that I'm going to be 39 in July, and I had a baby at 37, so this is just what life is going to be like. But the more I told myself that was the case, the more depressed I got trying to imagine that this was life from here on out. This cannot be me forever.

Two of the friends I traveled with have a dependency on Diet Coke to get her through each day. They started first thing in the morning. One of the girls takes either a caffeine pill or drinks an energy drink a couple of times a day. I don't want to go that route because I can't imagine there aren't long-term ramifications, but I am close to doing it myself because I see what they are accomplishing in a day, and I am envious of their energy.

My poor husband is at his wit's end. He has begged me to contact you for weeks now. I have put it off in hopes that I could find a local doctor that I can work with. But now I am in a place where I desperately need help, and I just don't like asking for it.

Any advice you could give me would be greatly appreciated.

(Name withheld)

The sad thing is this is not an uncommon occurrence in women today. Seventy-two percent of the women that come into our clinic are taking antidepressants. By their own admission, taking antidepressants makes them become "numb." But then again, what are they supposed to do? They've been to their doctor, had blood tests run, and "everything looks good," they're told.

As authors, we debated even including this chapter in our book. But even the title *I Am More than Enough* can be a mirage if you physically don't feel good. That woman in the above letter was voicing what literally thousands of women are experiencing, and these women are finding little to no answers from the current medical paradigm.

We would like to give you some advice, which we trust will give you hope. You *can* feel better. You *can* have the vitality and energy you seek but not by taking drugs that alter your thinking, and probably not by eating the way you are eating.

OUT OF BALANCE, OUT OF CONTROL

My wife and I [Robert] were driving down the freeway one day when she asked, "What's that noise?"

"What noise? I don't hear anything," I said.

"That noise!" she whispered, and we both listened intently.

"I still don't hear anything. What are you hearing?"

"*That* noise. Can't you hear it?"

When we finally stopped for gas, I nonchalantly walked around the car. There it was: the right front tire was worn on the inside tread—down to bare steel rim! I was shocked. I had to admit to my wife that she wasn't crazy.

I didn't dare even drive the car after that. We actually put two new tires on the car after rotating them all.

Here is the point of this story: our car was so out of balance that it was dangerous. If we'd had a blowout at seventy miles per hour, we would have probably gone out of control and may have been killed. Out of balance—out of control.

That is exactly where so many women are today, out of balance . . . with their hormones. We cannot emphasize enough the importance of getting your hormones evaluated. Let's look at some of the issues that occur when one or more of your hormones are out of balance.

Thyroid: the thyroid gland runs your entire metabolism. Every cell of your body is affected by this hormone. It affects not only your physical capabilities but also your mental capabilities. Here are some of the most common symptoms associated with low thyroid levels:

- Chronic fatigue/constant lethargy
- Inability to lose weight despite dieting and exercising
- Dry skin and other skin problems
- Cold hands and feet
- Female hair thinning/loss
- Extreme mood swings/irritability
- Anxiety/panic attacks
- Depression
- Heel cracking
- Constipation
- Brain fog

Do any of these sound familiar? How do you think you'll feel about yourself (your self-image) when you have many of those above symptoms? We agree.

Now comes the problem we hear from women almost everyday in our clinic: "But my doctor ran blood tests and said my thyroid was *normal*."

There can be three reasons for this. First, and most commonly, your doctor only ran what is called a *TSH test* (thyroid stimulating hormone). This is totally insufficient to establish whether your thyroid is underactive. Other tests must be run in order to find out if you are hypothyroid—or if you have autoimmune thyroid problems (both of which have fatigue and anxiety as common symptoms). Second, another possibility is that they did run some of the needed tests and said you are in the "low normal" range. "Low normal"? What does that mean? Does that mean you get to live the rest of your life as a "low normal" person? Many doctors will wait for you to drop well below the "low normal" range before they will do anything about it. This, in our opinion, is unacceptable, and it is frustrating for you.

Third, many women come to our clinic already taking thyroid—synthetic thyroid—and it is not working for them. So their doctor increased the dose: still no changes, but they can still make you "wired but tired." Tired during the day, and wired during the night when you should be sleeping soundly. And chances are good that you'll be over-weight. More frustration.

Progesterone: This female hormone is made by your ovaries. It is critical for mental *and* physical well-being. It is a powerful mood lifter. Here are some of the issues you could be facing when your progesterone levels are low (and this could begin as a teenager):

- Insomnia (both falling asleep and staying asleep)
- PMS issues (irritability, weepiness, short fuse before your period)
- Menstrual problems (painful cramping, excessive bleeding, irregular timing), endometriosis
- Panic/anxiety attacks
- Depression
- Breast cancer/heart disease
- Osteoporosis (thinning of the bones)
- Infertility/miscarriages/postpartum depression/severe morning sickness

The problem here is that most doctors will never check your progesterone levels. This is sad, because as you see, it affects so many things going on in a woman's body. Modern medicine's answer to progesterone is to prescribe antidepressants or birth control pills. Neither of those are good long-term solutions. They may help temporarily, but in the long run, they have so many side effects that they become risky.

Adrenal glands: Your adrenal glands are located on top of each of your kidneys. They are the hormone glands in your body that help you deal with stress. They are essential to maintaining proper energy levels and overall drive.

- Feelings of being emotionally "burnt out."
- Low blood pressure
- Light-headedness when arising quickly
- Allergies
- Asthma
- Difficulty getting out of bed in the morning followed by fatigue the entire day.
- Relentless sugar and salt cravings.

When the adrenals are not functioning properly, they can affect all the other hormones in the body, dragging you down to total burn-out physically and mentally. At that point, Icy can tell you anything and you'll believe it! When was the last time your doctor tested your adrenals? Or even mentioned them?

Estrogen: This is the hormone of menopause. Too much estrogen can cause what is called "estrogen dominance." Women with estrogen levels that are too high with respect to progesterone complain that they have turned into "the Wicked Witch of the West." Estrogen levels that are too low can cause:

- Osteoporosis
- Hot flashes
- Night sweats
- Vaginal dryness
- Insomnia
- Saggy, wrinkly skin
- Low sex drive

Too much or too little—a balance of estrogen and progesterone are critical for feeling good, and feeling good about yourself.

Testosterone: Most women think that this is for men only—that women don't need it. This is not true at all. It is essential for women to have it—just not as much as a man. When we prescribe testosterone for a man, we will usually give him about two hundred milligrams per day. A woman may need only two to ten milligrams per day. Most women that we test have low testosterone. Here are some of the problems low testosterone will cause in a woman:

- Low or no sex drive
- Loss of muscle tone (sagging muscles), even if you are working out daily
- Osteoporosis
- Depression
- Loss of assertiveness, that is, becoming passive or unresponsive about life
- Loss of feelings of well-being

Insulin: We could go on and on about this hormone and its importance in your life. Our country has become a nation of high insulin levels. If you doctor has never talked to you about this hormone, you need to find out about it. It is the number-one reason a person becomes overweight, and the number one reason a person cannot lose weight, despite dieting and exercising regularly. It is beyond the scope of this book to go into any depth on the matter, but you need to keep your insulin low if you are overweight.

Insulin promotes inflammation all over the human body. The term "insulin resistance" is crucial for you to understand. Insulin's nickname is "the fat-storing hormone." You must realize that you can never lose weight and keep it off if your insulin levels are out of balance.

Let us give you an example of what you are eating every day is affecting your insulin:

Rachel is forty-two years old and leads a very active lifestyle. She is five foot six and weighs 165 pounds. Rachel has been concerned about her weight and has dieted and exercised so much over the last ten years without results that she is sick of the whole thing. She has given up. Rachel needs to know how insulin is the culprit. Here is a conversation with her, which you may find to be revealing:

Dr. Jones: "So, Rachel, you are concerned about your weight. Tell me, do you eat a pretty healthy diet?"

Rachel: "Yes, I am very careful about what I eat."

Dr. Jones: "Great. So tell me, what did you have for breakfast this morning?"

Rachel: "Uh, let's see. I had a banana, a piece of seven-grain whole wheat toast, and a glass of fresh-squeezed orange juice."

Dr. Jones: "Okay. What did you have yesterday for breakfast?"

Rachel: "Yesterday I had a bowl of oatmeal. Steel-cut oats, with milk and a little honey for a sweetener."

(At this point it was obvious what was going on. Rachel thinks she is eating a healthy diet, but she is not—not if she wants to lose her belly fat and the weight around her hips.)

Dr. Jones: "Are those typical breakfasts for you?"

Rachel: "Yes, and I do eat some cold cereal if I'm in a hurry."

Dr. Jones: "Well, Rachel, now I know why you can't lose a pound, even if you exercise every day. All you're eating for breakfast is *sugar!*"

Rachel: "Oh, no. I don't eat sugar. I'm very careful to avoid treats and desserts."

What Rachel doesn't understand is that she *is* eating sugar, lots of sugar. She just doesn't realize it. She thinks that as long as she doesn't eat cookies, candies, cakes, donuts, ice cream, and chocolate, she isn't eating any sugar. Wrong!

Orange juice? Oatmeal? Cold cereal? Milk? Seven-grain wheat bread? Banana? *It's all sugar—and it makes her insulin go up.* Do you remember what insulin's nickname is? It's called the "fat-storing hormone." Even though Rachel thinks she is eating healthy food, she is not—not if she wants good energy levels and not if she wants to lose fat. High insulin levels will lock fat into your fat cells and prevent that fat from ever being burned, even if you exercise.

And here is a frightening fact: eating carbs for breakfast (without balancing them by eating proteins and good fats) can elevate insulin levels *for the next seventy-two hours*! That means everything she eats for the next seventy-two hours could be converted to fat for long-term storage—on her tummy and hips.

Rachel could hardly believe what she was hearing. "Why didn't my doctor tell me that a long time ago? All I eat are carbs, except at dinner when I eat some meat. So what am I supposed to eat?"

Here is the answer to her question and the "core truth" that you need to understand: the healthier the insulin level you achieve, the thinner you will become and the better energy and higher state of well-being you will have.

Carbohydrates, starches, sugar. They are all the same when it comes to being overweight. If you are insulin resistant, your body can't tell the difference between a candy bar and a baked potato. For the insulin-resistant person, a glass of apple juice would be much more "fattening" than a piece of deep-fried chicken! The apple juice is pure sugar. The chicken has no sugar (although we suggest you fry it in a healthy fat—not a "junk" fat)—it's mainly protein. Proteins and good fats are key to helping you not only lose weight—but also controlling your blood sugar levels. If you tend to be hypoglycemic (low blood sugar), you need to be careful about getting enough protein and good fat in your diet and not constantly spiking your insulin levels with carbohydrates and starches.

This is not just a matter of losing those extra twenty pounds. This is a matter of having good energy levels on a consistent basis. When your energy is low, are you *more than enough?* Most likely not. Then Icy comes in and tells you all the things you have done wrong that day, and you don't have the brain energy enough to talk back to her. You lose the battle before it's even begun. Low energy = low resistance = low self-worth. Large fluctuations in blood sugar levels during the day make you prone to mental fatigue, exhaustion, short fuse, and irritability. Then how do you feel about yourself?

CONCLUSION

Get your hormone levels checked by a competent doctor who deals with hormones. If you go to your family doctor, and he or she says, "I don't think you have any hormonal problems," you may have to insist that they check the hormones that we listed at the beginning of this chapter. When the blood tests come back and the doctor says, "Everything looks normal," you may want to get a second opinion, preferably by an endocrinologist.

The ranges in the lab tests would suggest that unless you "have one foot in the grave" you are okay. Here's an example: the range for thyroid (the free T3 it's called) is anywhere from 420 all the way down to 230. If you are at 240 are you in the *normal* range? Yes, of course you are. But how do you feel? Terrible? Then is 240 a good level for you? No! But your doctor is waiting for you to drop below 240. Then they might do something. Or they may suggest that "we wait and see." Or they may suggest an antidepressant. That is not the answer. These are hormonal imbalances that we see in our clinic every day, and unless these imbalances are addressed, *you'll never feel better*. Trust us on this. Our clinic is filled with frustrated, tired, over-whelmed women who are just looking to feel some hope about their health and energy. The modern medical system could be failing you. Get answers now.

Remember: Out of Balance, Out of Control. Are you out of control?

WE DARE YOU

We dare you to go get your hormones checked if you're experiencing dragging, sagging, or nagging. If you need hormonal balancing, tell your doctor that you would prefer to use bioidentical hormone therapy, not traditional synthetic hormones that have side effects.

Request a blood test that includes all of the above hormones. If you want to see which particular hormones may be causing problems for you, go to www.utahwellnessinstitute.com and click on the "Learning Media" tab. This can change your life.

eighteen

Pen-Purging

We have given you many tools in this book to help you overcome the tendency to be self-critical. We give you one more here: *the pen-purge.*

This tool is so effective, it can, by itself, nearly eliminate the propensity of women to be down on themselves. Combined with the other tools in this book, there is no real reason you have to go on suffering from low self-worth. As always the caveat: tools don't work if left on the tool bench unused.

Edward Bulwer-Lytton said, "The pen is mightier than the sword." Indeed, for the purpose of creating the self-directed change we are seeking in this book, your pen *is* your sword—the sword of change. The act of merely writing words on a page can create changes in your brain. It can heal wounds created by parents, friends, or siblings from when you were a child. It can give you power to overcome. It can change you forever, one word at a time.

A DIARY VS. A JOURNAL

What's the difference between a diary and a journal? Plenty. A diary is essentially reporting what happened to you on a particular day. It is filled with "objective stuff" like a newspaper reporter detailing the scene of a crime. Reporters are directed to give just the facts. "Don't let your emotions show in the article," the editor says. "Remain impartial."

Journaling is much different. It doesn't necessarily just catalogue facts or events. It is self-exploration, self-expression. You write what you *feel* about what happened—not *what* happened.

Now before you say, "Oh brother. They want us to write our feelings. Blah, blah, blah." *Please*, hear us out on this subject. It will make all the difference in you getting rid of Women's Weakness. It will help you get out of the funnel, or not even jump into the funnel in the first place. Wouldn't it be nice to be in full control of your feelings regarding who you are?

So read on and look at the evidence.

"EXPRESSIVE WRITING"

We would like to introduce you to a University of Texas professor/researcher/psychologist named James Pennebaker. Dr. Pennebaker began his fascinating research back in the 1970s. He studied people who had gone through various traumatic events such as sexual abuse, physical abuse, unexpected spousal deaths, brain injuries, and other events in peoples' past that were still causing them pain even years after the events transpired.

One of the first things to come out of his research was the fact that people in these trauma studies that kept it all a secret had much higher risk of major and minor illnesses. Really? Yes, the fact that they never divulged their past traumas had an affect on their physical health and well being.

He then decided to see if people who *wrote* about these past traumatic events would have better outcomes as those who merely talked about them. He found it to be true.[1]

Further studies by Dr. Pennebaker, later published in medical journals, found that writing only twenty minutes per day about their traumatic events for no more than four days actually directly affected their immune systems.[2]

In April 1999 a study called "Effects of Writing About Stressful Experiences on Symptom Reduction in Patients With Asthma or Rheumatoid Arthritis" was published in the Journal of the American Medical Association. The subjects were told to write about the most stressful event of their lives for twenty minutes for only three days. The conclusion of the study was, "These gains were beyond those attributable to the standard medical care that all participants were receiving."

An editorial opinion by David Spiegel in the same issue said, "Were the authors to have provided similar outcome evidence about a new drug, it likely would be in widespread use within a short time."[3]

Dr. Pennebaker did another intriguing study with men who had lost their jobs without notice after being employed by tech companies for years. Pennebaker said about these men, they were "the most angry, hostile, unpleasant bunch I ever worked with." During the study, one group of those men was asked to write about their most personal feelings and reflections about their predicament. The other group was asked to write about what they were doing daily since they had been unemployed. Eight months later the study ended. They had all gone through approximately the same number of job interviews, but the difference was that over half the men who had written about their feelings were now gainfully employed, while a mere 20 percent of the other group was employed. Dr. Pennebaker conjectured that, in writing came the healing: their anger about the whole job loss nearly disappeared.[4]

Later studies showed that people with cancer were impacted positively by just writing small amounts about the trauma of having cancer.

Here are Pennebaker's instructions that he would give participants:

> Over the next four days, I want you to write about your deepest emotions and thoughts about the most upsetting experience in your life. Really let go and explore your feelings and thoughts about it. In your writing, you might tie this experience to your childhood, your relationship with your parents, people you have loved or love now, or even your career. How is this experience related to who you would like to become, who you have been in the past, or who you are now?[5]

PEN-PURGING

Now just how does this apply to the issues of low self-worth? We want you to use your pen to "purge" your thoughts onto paper. Call it "journaling" if you wish to, but we like the term *pen-purging*. It's much more descriptive of what it will feel like. Purging is eliminating, cleansing, or removing.

First, the act of actually writing something forces the brain to think actively. We cannot write without thinking. Also, in our experience, we find better results with actually using a pen and a simple notebook, rather than a computer. Why? The actual physical act of writing the words seems to make greater impressions on the brain than using keystrokes on a laptop. So we suggest that you buy a simple spiral notebook or journal and get a nice pen and put it in your own handwriting. There is something about seeing your own writing that is much more meaningful than printed text.

What are you going to write about? Obviously, whatever happened that day with regards to your self-worth issues.

- "Today I felt like a martyr." Write about it.
- "Yesterday, before I went to work, I put my Shield up and it worked all day long!" How did it work? What happened?
- "Today I was so down on myself." Write your feelings.
- "Tonight Icy was so loud; she wouldn't shut up." Write what you did.
- "I yelled at the kids so much today. I'm a terrible mother." Admit it, and put it in your journal.
- "I walked into that meeting and immediately felt inferior. I should have done my 'Self-scan' but I didn't." Why didn't you? Tell yourself on paper.
- "Saturday Tom treated me so rudely at the store. I realized at that very moment that it wasn't about me. He was really down on himself. I felt like I had this huge breakthrough!" Do a Pen Purge!
- "I already knew going into that building that I would get triggered. I set myself up. I should have seen it coming." Tell yourself about it all on paper.

By writing about it for even ten minutes, you get to monitor your thinking and your actions. You get to dissect what you did and how it made you feel. You reflect on it. What you are looking for is the truth about the event or trauma. This is virtual training . . . in the mind's eye. You are reliving the events, and in reliving you can see what is *really* happening inside your mind. This is when control starts. You begin to look at things and your feelings from a completely different angle. It is as if you get to have an out-of-body experience, seeing the event in an altered state of mind.

There are your words on paper. "Did I *really* think that?" Writing the words is like holding up an ornately carved and painted Hummel figurine right in front of your face. You turn it around, examining from all points of view. You notice things on the figurine that you have never noticed before, even though it's been sitting on your shelf for fifteen years.

So it is with pen-purging. The very act of getting the words from your mind to paper is training. It is healing and enlightening. You'll hear yourself saying, "I can't believe it. That event has *nothing* to do with who I am." Or, "Wow, I can't believe how easily I got hooked by her. It wasn't *her* at all. It was all in *my* mind. My thinking was disgusting, but now I see it—I see how quickly it happened to me."

As you put pen to paper, your thoughts from the day are transposed to words. Those words, when written down, go into "the mind's eye" and start affecting your brain. You begin to reprogram your default setting by writing about the *feelings and emotions* you experienced during the day. Write about how you *really* feel, and not so much about how you *think* you should feel.

You went down the funnel all the way to beating yourself up? Great! Write about it. The junior high principal called and said your daughter was caught skipping out of class and was found at the mall, and you went back to your old default setting, telling yourself what a failure of a parent you are? Good. Put it down on paper. Purge. The act of writing will help you see the truth about the whole thing.

Your best friend drove over to your house to show you her new birthday present from her husband: a brand-new Mercedes. You immediately went into comparison mode. For the next couple of hours, you couldn't get it out of your mind that your old sedan with the fading paint job means, of course, that you are a loser. Ha! Do a pen-purge about it that night as you sit on your bed.

The writing is for nobody else's eyes. Only *you* will ever read this, so you can be *completely* honest with yourself. Of course literally *all* of us would be embarrassed to have somebody read our pen-purge journal, so it is *critical* that you free yourself of that thought by knowing that you are going to destroy these writings. As Pennebaker told his students, plan on throwing these writings away, burning them, shredding them, or whatever you want.⁶ Some people reread them; some destroy them. It doesn't matter. It's the process of writing that is the catharsis. One of our focus group women said that pen-purging was like "vomiting all over her journal." She put all the ugly truth on paper.

But curious things happen. During the pen-purging process, clarity begins to distill into the mind. The truth begins to start slowly emerging. You begin seeing things the way they really are. Truth has a way of doing that to us all. We begin to see the lies that we are telling ourselves or that the world around us tells us. Your daughter's three-day suspension from school has nothing to do with your personal worth. Maybe your friend needs a Mercedes to feel good about herself—or maybe her *husband* needs it to feel good about *himself.* It's not for you to judge; it's for you to get your feelings purged onto paper, and let that start changing your brain.

Pen-purging will bring personal understanding. You will learn more about yourself by doing it than nearly any other activity in which you are engaged. It will cause you to reflect over and over again on the events of the day as you "vomit all over the journal." You'll have some good laughs at yourself, as in the "I can't believe I got triggered so easily this morning," and you'll have some good cries, as in the "Am I making any progress with my life—*at all?*"

Pen-purging forces thinking. Thinking forces growth and change.

The "magic" if you will, is that the moment you put pen to paper you are training for the next days' events. You are putting on your armor, your Shield. You are going in battle more mentally and emotionally prepared for what ever comes your way the next day.

Pen-purging: it's the secret sauce!

WE DARE YOU

We dare you to buy a small journal or simple spiral notebook within the next three days. Review this chapter and simply start pen-purging. It will amaze you! Do it every night for at least two weeks. Let it become a new ten-minute habit. It's just between you and yourself, no one else. Laugh, cry, grow, become.

NOTES

1. "Writing to Heal," University of Texas in Austin, updated March 15, 2005, accessed April 2013, http://www.utexas.edu/features/2005/writing.

2. James Pennebaker, *Writing to Heal: A Guided Journal for Recovering from Trauma and Emotional Upheaval* (Oakland, California: New Harbinger, 2004).

3. D. Spiegel "Healing words: emotional expression and disease outcome." *JAMA* 281, no. 14 (1999): 1328–29, as quoted in Gunaratnam, *Narrative and Stories in Health Care: Illness, Dying and Bereavement* (New York: Oxford University Press, 2009)

4. S. Spera et al., "Expressive Writing and Coping with Job Loss," *Academy of Management Journal* 37, no. 3 (1994): 722–33, accessed May 2013, http://homepage.psy.utexas.edu/homepage/faculty/pennebaker/reprints/Spera.pdf.

5. James Pennebaker, "Writing and Health: Some Practical Advice," accessed April 2013, http://homepage.psy.utexas.edu/homepage/faculty/pennebaker/home2000/WritingandHealth.html.

6. Ibid.

conclusion

In the introduction to this book, we said that some of the things in the book could be painful; that there would be no "fluff" in the book. Men's Weakness—Women's Weakness is pretty potent stuff, but if our intent is to have you look inside your mind and really recognize what is going on, and we actually get you to do that, we have accomplished part of our intent. Getting you to actually *do* will be up to you, the individual reader.

Dennis Prager, in his book *Happiness Is a Serious Problem*, observes,

> Interestingly, women are rarely said to have a midlife crisis. I think that there are two primary reasons for this. One is that women generally do not bank their identity on achievement as much as men do—not being president of something does not cause depression in most women. The other reason is that women tend to have a whole-life crisis. This is not meant critically. Given women's generally more in-tune-with-reality nature, it is not surprising that they would be plagued throughout life with feelings that men don't tend to confront until their middle years.[1]

That "whole-life crisis" is exactly what we are aiming at in this book. We have described the problem. We have given you tools. We have dared you. We have nearly pleaded with you to train, not just try. Now it's up to you. If you are the type of person who quickly reads through a book to "see what it's all about first," that's fine. But now go back and use the tools. Change your default settings. Stop allowing yourself to get triggered all day long. Put up your Shield. Do the Self Scan all day long if you need to. Use CSG. Pen-purging is almost miraculous. Don't take our word for it. Don't try it. Train with it.

Go further than just having your "battle buddy" read this book. If you have daughters, lend it to them. Then discuss it together. No woman is immune from Women's Weakness. But having the tools to deal with it can bring more happiness and contentment than you have ever dreamed of.

Remember Margaret? She was eighty-four when she said she was no longer plagued with feelings of low self-worth. You cannot wait that long to change your thinking about yourself. It just isn't necessary, either.

You can change. You can experience a personal, inner revolution in how you feel about yourself, because, the truth of it is, you are *more* than enough.

Use the tools.

NOTES

1. Dennis Prager, *Happiness Is a Serious Problem* (New York: HarperCollins Publishers, 1998), 27.

about the authors

Robert B. Jones was born and raised in the Pacific Northwest. He received his undergraduate degree in interpersonal communications and speech from Brigham Young University. He did graduate studies at Portland State University in biochemistry and his doctorate at University of Western States in Portland, Oregon, and he has served as a faculty member in the past. Dr. Jones has been in clinical practice for over thirty-two years. Currently his practice is limited to bioidentical hormone therapy for women and men. He has appeared on ABC News, NBC News, and other local television programs. He practices in Draper, Utah, and is the clinical director of the Utah Wellness Institute. He is married to Joy D. Harmon, and they are the parents of five children and grandparents of thirteen grandchildren. He is an avid reader, speaker, and mountain biker.

Bryce Dunford has been a religious educator for twenty years. He has taught thousands of students both at the high school and college levels in Utah and Arizona.

He received a bachelor's degree in human biology from the University of Utah and a master's degree in educational leadership from Northern Arizona University. He and his wife, Jennifer, reside in South Jordan, Utah, and have nine children.